MY FAITH IN IMMORTALITY

MY FAITH
IN IMMORTALITY

By

WILLIAM E. BARTON

AUTHOR OF
The Life of Abraham Lincoln

INDIANAPOLIS
THE BOBBS-MERRILL COMPANY
PUBLISHERS

Printed in the United States of America

PRINTED AND BOUND
BY BRAUNWORTH & CO., INC.
BROOKLYN, NEW YORK

PREFACE

The only reason which need be given for the writing of this book is the clear conviction of the author, out of a long experience, that one of the profound needs of the present time is a faith in immortality, reasonable, intelligible and free from superstition. Such a faith this book endeavors to assist.

This volume was written for the comfort of others, and not to express any personal sorrow on the part of the author. From such sorrow his own life had been relatively free. A thousand times he had stood beside the grave. For forty years he had preached to others a gospel of comfort, and during that whole time death had not entered his own door. On the morning of November 7, 1925, when the final touches were put on the manuscript, and the wrapped package lay upon the desk awaiting the expressman to convey it to the publisher, no shadow was seen to impend above his own home. Before the day ended, the wife of his youth, well beloved for forty happy years, lay dead. While no page of this book was written as an expression of the author's own grief, the proofsheets have been read in the shadow of a great personal bereavement. The faith which he has preached to others, the faith which she cherished, is the author's own comfort. If the pure in heart see God, hers is a radiant vision.

W. E. B.

CONTENTS

MY FAITH IN IMMORTALITY

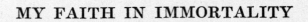

MY FAITH
IN IMMORTALITY

CHAPTER I

I WONDER

I FIND myself living in a highly improbable world. I was not consulted in advance about the matter of my coming here to live. If I had been, I think I should have come. I am certainly glad I am here. I am glad of every year I have lived, and glad that I still am living. I am in no haste to leave; if I could continue to live for another hundred years as happily as I have lived for something less than my first hundred, I should be willing to sign on the dotted line an agreement to accept the added century and more of life in this world, and I should be happy in the prospect. On the other hand, I am not mourning on account of the improbability of such an opportunity. I am here, and glad I came, and content to stay as long as I can be happy and useful, and then move on.

It is not the kind of world I should have made or expected. I have never admitted that I could have made a better one, but it has sometimes seemed to me that, although professional optimists, of whom I am almost one, may declare that this is the best of all possible worlds, it might have been possible to "mold it nearer to the heart's desire." It certainly is not a perfect world. Some of us have spent a good many years serving as members of charitable, educational and philanthropic committees trying to make it better, and I expect to keep on doing so. Meantime, I do not complain, but I wonder.

When I speak of this world, I do not mean this ponderable globe, but that part of it which enters into my experience and vision, plus whatever I am able to know and see in the limited part of the visible universe that I happen to notice and think about. This world, so limited and defined, is filled with material for wonder. If I were mapping the constellations, I should not be content to imagine that one group of stars outlined a bear and another a scorpion and another a pair of twins; I should look around until I found a few stars that might make for me an interrogation point.

It is not alone the stars that cause me to wonder. I find equal cause for wonder in much smaller and nearer objects. I can say with Tennyson, that if I understood all the answers to all the questions and wonderments that are conjured up by the "flower in the crannied wall," I should know the whole story of the universe. Tennyson did not know; he wondered. I do not know; I wonder.

I must not cheapen this word "wonder." It must not be used for mere conjecture or superficial uncertainty. I must not say, "I wonder when George will come," or, "It is a wonder the baby did not break his arm when he fell downstairs." George will come when he comes; I should like to know when, but that is not a matter for wonder. I am glad the baby was hurt no worse, but, given the baby's height and weight and the density of his tissues and the flexibility of his cartilaginous bones and the thickness of the stair carpet, it was not possible for the baby to be either more or less hurt than he was. We must save the word "wonder" for things that are really wonderful. For these lesser matters a cheaper word will suffice.

I wonder what is the nature of matter. This table is made of oak, and this book of paper, with a cover of cloth; the electric light is a matter of glass globe and copper wire; but what is the basic reality that inheres in wood and paper and cloth and glass and copper and mountains and mole-hills and constellations and nebulæ and other things? What is the common element inherent in and inclusive of all these and other materials? I have read various learned treatises in reply to this inquiry. I am not unfamiliar with certain theories of realism and idealism behind which the philosophers and scientists have concealed a pitiful scrap of their ignorance. I am not asking for the fig leaf of their nomenclature, nor the assumption that when a Greek word is made into a scientific name the question is answered. I also know Greek, or once did, and can make names to hide my own ignorance; but I am here and now confessing it, and with it I am confessing the ignorance of all the

14

others. All of us together do not know a millionth part of one per cent of what there is that might be known. We do not "guess at half and multiply by two." We guess at a millionth and there are not figures enough for a denominator of our ignorance. What is matter? Or, to use a plural noun with a singular verb as the Greeks sometimes did, what is things?*

Our definition of particular things is a summary of certain perceived qualities: "The rose is red; the violet is blue; sugar is sweet," and so on.

But the quality of redness is not in the rose. The petals of the rose are so constituted as to reflect to the eye certain red rays of light. These rays are absorbed and not reflected by the leaves, which are therefore called by another color. But when we say that the leaves of the rose-bush are green and the petals red, or that the grass is green, and that the sky is blue, we know better than to suppose that we are speaking of qualities eternally inherent in the leaf and petal, grass and sky. I have seen

---

*There is a little book of popular essays for young people, issued in England in 1911, the author apparently a physician, entitled *I Wonder*. It was published by Macmillan, and if still in print may be read with profit. I can not think it had a large sale, as I have seen only one copy, which I have.

grass that was not green, and yet was undeniably grass; and I have seen the sky when it was not blue. The color of the sky and the color of the grass are in the eye that receives reflected rays of light of those particular colors. I do not know what the real color of the grass or sky is. I wonder.

Yet, if that were the whole of the problem, I could afford to let it go, and for practical purposes, I do not consider it. The green of the grass, and the blue of the sky are "good enough for me." But when I am seeking to know what things is (not what particular thing as distinct from other things, *are* but what all things *is*) I must not let myself be deceived by appearances which I know are deceptive. I wonder what is the nature of matter.

I learned years ago that matter is composed of molecules, and that molecules are made up of homogeneous and indivisible units, far too small for the microscope to disclose, and called by a Greek name "atoms" which simply means "can-not-be-cut." But now I am told that each atom is a solar system with a central positive electron and a number of negative electrons moving about it. I am willing to believe it, though it requires great faith.

16

But I do not know yet what matter is or what things is. I wonder.

I live in a world of movement and energy, which seems to move more or less by method. If I eat a peach and toss the stone out of my window, I do so in expectation that outside the window, where the force of my arm conveys it, the stone will be taken in charge by another form of energy, which doubtless is operative inside the window as well as out, and that the stone will not keep on going in the direction in which I toss it, and will not fall up, but will fall down to the ground and disappear harmlessly among the pine needles. By way of expressing my expectation that it will fall down and not up I say that the law of gravitation pulls it down. This is as good a way of disposing of the subject as any, and it disposes of the troublesome question very much as I dispose of the peach-stone, by giving it a name and tossing it out of the window. But if I cared to plant the peach-stone I might observe other forces than gravitation at work. What is force? Yes, I wonder what kind of force that is which we call life.

The wonder of life! I have seen it come and

17

go—the flower bursting from the bud; the seed pushing through the turf and struggling to the light; the bird picking its shell, and I wonder. Who told the seed that if it pushed through the soil it would find light? Who told the bird that picking was the way to get out? Who told the bird that there *was* any way out? I wonder, I wonder!

I wonder what that force is which is not convertible into any other force, yet which is one of the mightiest of all the forms of energy—the force of life. I am not entering into any biological discussion as to vitalism and the various forms of negation or qualification which some of them employ. I wonder what life is. I wonder what mind is!

I pause for a moment to listen to the comment of Mr. Gadgrind; "What's the use of wondering? All I wonder is where my next meal is coming from. All this talk about wonder seems to me unprofitable."

Go, Mr. Gadgrind, and get your next meal. But stay, even you must wait a little longer. This thing we call wonder is not so unprofitable as you suppose. If wonder is waste energy, why wonder about the meal? And if you are to wonder, why

18

not wonder about something greater? That clever, if sometimes wearisome essayist, Chesterton, was never more true than when he said, "The world will never starve for want of wonders, but only for want of wonder." When Emerson said that "wonder is the seed of science," he was hardly more than paraphrasing Socrates, whom Plato quotes as having said that "wonder is the sole beginning of philosophy."

Wonder is one of the most precious things in the world. It is the foundation of knowledge and the soul of all that can be called success. Even if you only wonder where you can sell another bushel of potatoes, you are turning a cheap form of wonder to profit. There are many men like the lout of whom Dryden wrote:

Long stood the noble youth oppressed with awe,
And stupid at the wondrous things he saw.

We shall not be quite so stupid if we have mind enough to wonder. Among those extra-canonical "sayings" of Jesus which have some degree of right to be considered genuine utterances of the Lord, is one that reads, "He that wonders shall reign; and he that reigns shall rest."

How long am I to wonder in this fashion? I could go on forever, wondering, wondering; but I should like to wonder as profitably as possible. The world in which I live has been created with great ingenuity, apparently to make me wonder.

No one of the fundamental mysteries has ever been removed. The mystery of matter, the mystery of time and space, the mystery of life, the mystery of mind, the mysteries of pain and death, all are with us as they have been always. Nor is there any relief in turning from the mysteries of vast proportions or immeasurable distances to those that are smaller in bulk or closer at hand. A recent minor poet has thus written of the cloud in the sky and the flower in her hand:

I see the giant stalking in the sky,
The giant cloud above the wilderness,
Bearing a mystery too far, too high
    For my poor guess.
Away I turned me, saying, "I must seek
In lowlier places for the wonder-word.
Something more little, intimate, shall speak."
    A bright rose stirred.
And long I looked into its face to see
At last some hidden import of the hour.
And I had thought to turn from mystery,
    But O, flower! flower! —AGNES LEE.

There is no escape from mystery. But if we can not push it far from us, we may at least hope not to be crushed under its weight, or lie down in supine and hopeless refusal to think. If we do not accept the challenge which life's mysteries present to us, then, in the midst of life, we are in death.

I do not covet that frame of mind which permits a man to go through life seeing wonders and never wondering. I have no sympathy with the man who would yawn at witnessing the creation of the world if he were to see it a second time. The normal man will say with Wordsworth:

> My heart leaps up when I behold
>   A rainbow in the sky.
> So was it when my life began;
> So is it now I am a man;
> So be it when I shall grow old,
>   Or let me die.

The man without this sense of wonder need not pray to die, he is already dead. Within him something very precious has died for which nothing can compensate. I behold a rainbow or a dew-drop and I wonder.

I wonder at the infinitely great in nature, and the infinitely small. Everything is wonderful.

21

But let me instance just one more object of wonder.

I might wonder at the mystery of pain; I might wonder at the presence of evil in a world made by a good God. I do wonder about these things, but now especially I am wondering about death.

Long ago I stopped wondering about death as a fact in human experience.

I shall not argue about it now. It is here. It is a fact which sooner or later we shall all face. A man must either suffer many sorrows and then die, or die young. What is death, and why is it?

I wonder if there is life after death. I know that millions of men and women have asked the same question, some of them with less experience than I. For while I have never been dead, I have seen much of death. I have stood beside a thousand graves and tried to speak words of comfort to a thousand different groups of weeping friends. They have wondered, and have asked me again and again what I believe about life after death.

I have a faith that to me is unspeakably precious; it is of this faith I write.

"If a man die, shall he live again?"

I wonder; I also believe.

CHAPTER II

THE FOUNDATION OF KNOWLEDGE

IT IS affirmed by one of our poets that ignorance is sometimes bliss; if that be true, this should be a blissful world, for we are very ignorant. When we say we know a thing, we usually mean that we believe, hope, or imagine it is true. We have to assume something in order to have ground on which to stand while we begin to explore and investigate. But let us begin as nearly as possible at rock bottom. Apart from the things that we believe, hope, or imagine to be true, what do we know?

We do not know that there will be a to-morrow nor can we prove that there was a yesterday. It would trouble us to demonstrate that there is a to-day. For all that we can prove, the world was created this morning, or is not yet created.

Very well, then, let us begin by denying everything. Let us not admit that anything exists. We will not admit that there is a world or a Bible or a God or any matter or force or mind.

But stop; there evidently is mind. I can not deny everything without thinking, and where there is thought there must be a thinker. I am thinking, perhaps foolishly, but still thinking. When I say "I deny that I am here," I know that I affirm that I am here denying it. A famous philosopher named Descartes once began in that way, denying everything, that he might clear the ground and start at the bottom. He put his first affirmation in a brief Latin sentence, *Cogito, ergo sum.* "I think, therefore I am."

I *am!* What an affirmation! God said to Moses, "Go say to Pharaoh, I am hath sent me." And here I am, saying the same thing of myself, "I am." Let me make much of this brief moment of isolated glory, for it will not last long. For this quarter second of speculative thinking there is nothing else in the universe than a thinking, doubting, denying I. "I deny that I am, therefore I am." Alone on this dizzy pedestal of denial I stand, kicking it down in the very act that raises me to the top of it, and having to admit that my very denial is a declaration that my denial is untrue.

I can not deny everything without laughing myself out of court. "I think, therefore I am," and to think negatively is just as sure proof as to think affirmatively. I no longer say, "I deny, therefore I am," but, "I affirm, and in the act of affirmation I declare that I am here."

But immediately I am conscious that I am not alone. If I say, "I am here, and nothing else is," and as I write down my own existence as the one article of my creed, I reach for pen and paper and face the fact that pen and paper are just as tangibly present as I am, and so are the floor, the table, the chair, the window and the earth, the trees, the lake and the sky.

I need not stop to enumerate them—I am here and I am not alone. Let me go forward this one step, grouping everything outside myself into one category, yet even in that act finding that I can not wholly shut myself out of this other classification, and let me call this group of pen and paper and chair and table and earth and lake and sky by some elastic name, however inexact—I know that there is a world, and that I am in it and a part of it.

This did not take us long, but it goes over the essential ground which philosophers have to traverse when they speak of "the subjective" and "the objective." The baby makes the same discovery when he finds that the pink toes under his petticoat are a part of him in a sense in which the petticoat is not. He has made a profound discovery, the mutual limitations and essential relationships of the subjective and objective.

We are getting rather deep into metaphysics, and are willing. We can go no deeper, nor can any one else. We began by denying everything, and we have already come a far cry from that.

Now I discover that the not-me part of this world is divided into two parts, the like-me and the unlike-me parts.

I raked the falling leaves of late summer and filled a wheelbarrow with them. My little granddaughter stood by, expectant. She had reason to believe a free ride awaited her. She said, "Grandpa, the wheelbarrow is full; there is not room for one more leaf."

"There is room for just one more leaf," I said, as I caught her up and seated her on top. "There is room for a little leaf from the tree of life."

To which she responded, "This little leaf can walk and talk."

So it can, thank God! "We all do fade as a leaf," even as Isaiah said, but some leaves can walk and talk and some can not. My little grand-daughter, and her brother, and her father and mother, and her grandmother, all belong to the like-me class, and so do the butcher and the baker and the candlestickmaker and the iceman and the milkman and the school-teacher.

I am not the only one of my kind. I am not so eminent in my isolation as I thought. There is a world, I am a part of it, and I have company.

I am shut in a very beautiful prison, with five windows. There is a wide window I call sight, and one somewhat narrower but still of good width which I call hearing; another that I call touch; a narrow one that I call taste and a very tiny aperture that I call smell. All the knowledge I have of the world outside myself is gained through one or more of these five windows.

I can not see all of myself nor do any or all of my five senses constitute my best knowledge of what I call me. I do not think of myself as the man I have heard singing bass or talking about books and bagpipes and cabbages and kings, or the man I have seen in the glass, but as the man I know in my thinking and in my purposes and my emotions. I see a hollyhock that I planted, and I remember that I planted it; I admire its color and decide to plant another one. In this swift process I move in a vast threefold orbit. I think about the hollyhock, and feel a sense of joy in it; I make a plan about it, and in all these things relating to the hollyhock I know not only the flower but myself. I can think; I can enjoy; I can plan, and all these in my relation to so small a thing as a hollyhock.

We began by denying everything, and we are far enough along to admit the five senses, the processes of the mind, and the existence of things outside, some of which things are people. Some leaves on the tree of life can walk and talk. That is enough about things, including such things as myself. I am now ready to go further. I soon accept as undeniable axioms such declarations as these:

Out of nothing, nothing can come.

Every effect has a cause, and every effect becomes a cause. There may have been, and I think must have been, a first cause, but I do not see how there can ever be a last cause.

Things exist; something must always have existed.

That which first existed must have had in it the potency of all that now exists. Nothing can have evolved in the development of the universe which was not potentially present when the universe began.

Thinking did not begin with me, nor with other feeble thinkers like me. There has been thought from the beginning; there must be a great Thinker.

We may go further and say that the fact that there is love is proof of a great Lover.

I am writing these words on a typewriter. It has the name of the maker stamped on the front; but if there were no such name there, I should know that it had a maker. No one could make me believe that forty pounds of steel junk had been dumped into my study and that it climbed upon the table and made itself into a typewriter. The man who made this typewriter knew something about machinery; he knew the English alphabet; he made large, plain white letters on the black keys, and those letters correspond to letters on the type bars. This machine did not happen. It was made by some one who had in mind just such uses as I put it to.

Things do not happen. There is a cause for every effect.

There was a great First Cause.

There is a present Greatest Cause.

In different languages they call Him by different names.

In my country we call Him God.

I have no quarrel with people who prefer another name, but that is the name I shall use.

These are the facts we assume: That you and I are here; that I wrote this book and you are reading it; that we are both interested in the same problems of life and its meanings, and that we both believe in what we call the law of cause and effect and in a mighty and purposeful and friendly God.

I am giving this outline, not as a demonstration, but as a swift review of the processes by which I arrive at the beginnings of an inquiry into the question of life after death.

I have no purpose to argue with the reader, or to

force him to adopt my conclusions. I am not seeking to compel him to agree with me. I am simply trying to find ground solid enough and large enough for us both to stand upon while we consider the problem of life and death and the life to come.

CHAPTER III

FACT AND FAITH

IN THE world where we are resident we are confronted by certain undeniable facts. One of these is death. Each season the leaves fall and the grass withers in the frost. Those forms of vegetable life that live through the winter do not survive for many winters. Even the great trees of the high Sierras, the oldest forms of life upon this planet, live but a trifling thousand years or such a matter. The coal we burn is dead trees. The rocks under our feet are filled with fossils of life that existed uncounted centuries ago. The earth is a great graveyard.

As the leaves die, so do the birds and the beasts and the fishes. No single form of life on this globe continues in any one individual. Tennyson thought of Nature as careless of the individual but careful of the type:

So careful of the type? But no,
From scarpèd cliff and quarried stone,
She cries, "A thousand types are gone;
I care for nothing; all must go."

In one of his delightful poems, *Clover*, Sidney
Lanier gave utterance to a feeling which must
come now and then to every thoughtful man, as he
views the apparent remorselessness of the mechanism of life. He drew a charming picture of a
clover-field, and fancied every head of clover a human head, the head of an artist, a musician, a poet;
they were all blossoming beautifully when along
came that which he called the Course-of-Things:

Now comes the Course-of-things, shaped like an
      Ox,
Slow browsing o'er my hillside, ponderously—
The huge-brawned, tame and workful Course-of-
      things,
That hath his grass if earth be round or flat,
And hath his grass if empires plunge in pain,
Or faiths flash out. This cool, unasking Ox
Comes browsing o'er my hills and vales of Time,
And sicklewise, about my poets' heads,
And twists them in, all, Dante, Keats, Chopin,
Raphael, Lucretius, Omar, Angelo,
Beethoven, Chaucer, Schubert, Shakespeare, Bach,
And Buddha, in one sheaf—and champs and
      chews,

33

With slantly churning jaws, and swallows down;
Then slowly makes advance to futureward, one
    inch.

So many clover-heads gulped down! So little
progress!

When Christian missionaries made their way to
England in 597, and journeyed as far inland as
Northumberland, they came to the domain of King
Ethelbert. It was a serious question with the king
whether these men should be allowed to teach a religion different from that which had been taught
in the realm. It involved many religious, social
and political uncertainties. He called a council of
his nobles and chiefs. There was diversity of
opinion. Then an aged chief arose and said:
"The king will remember that now and then as the
king sits at night with his men, a little bird will fly
in at a window, and across the room, and out again
through an opposite window into the night. From
the darkness it comes, and into the darkness it goes,
and it is for a brief space only in the light between.
Such is the spirit of man. If these men can tell us
concerning it, whence it comes and whither it goes,
let us hear them."

34

They were heard. Britain heard their message. America heard it. Successive generations have heard it and there is need that they shall still hear. For the spirit of man continues to make its swift flight through the narrow interval of life between the two great areas of darkness and silence. If there be any voices that can tell us whence this life comes and whither it goes, let us listen to them.

Now in this world where death reigns in every domain of animal and vegetable life, as well as in the constitution of the planet itself, we find this remarkable fact, that there exists a belief in life beyond death. How, in such a world, could such an idea have entered any mind? The sum total of experience would appear to be against it. We need not be disturbed by the various forms which this belief takes, or the varying and contradictory reasons which men give for their belief that death is not the end of life. It may be that one man believes that this world is so well governed that another world is implied in the very goodness of this one, while another may believe that this world is so bad that another world is necessary to adjust the dislocations and staggering inequalities of this:

35

both believe in immortality. We are not concerned with which gives the better reason for it, or whether either reason is good. Perhaps we might even say that the worse their logic the better for the purpose of our present inquiry. Men of widely different views on different and related matters somehow agree in their faith that there is life after death.

Nor is it anything adverse to our present inquiry that in all nations men shape their heaven in accordance with the condition of their own life on earth; it would be very natural that it should be so. If the Eskimo could be shown to believe in a heaven of hot fires and abundant whale-blubber, and a Hottentot in a heaven of snowdrifts and ice cream soda, their beliefs would still be of present interest, not for the correctness or incorrectness of their mental pictures of heaven, but for the fact that both these people believe in a heaven of some kind. We are not now seeking to determine how far any nation or tribe or sect holds the most rational or worthy idea of life after death; we are content with the discovery that such belief is very general.

Ralph Waldo Emerson said:

I have heard that wherever the name of man is spoken, the doctrine of immortality is announced; it cleaves to his constitution.

It has been affirmed by some but denied by others, that no nation or tribe has been found that does not believe in life after death. Whether the belief is absolutely universal is not of great importance; it would be very strange if it were so. Personally, I should be surprised if it were so, and I think it quite possible there are tribes so low in intellectual and spiritual development that no such belief exists among them. I could not name such a tribe and say that I knew it to be so. I think I have not visited any tribe of which this might be affirmed. Having sailed around the world and back again, I do not remember having encountered any people who did not believe in a hereafter. The simple American Indian burying a bow and arrows with the dead warrior for use in the happy hunting-ground, and the Pharaohs of Egypt erecting pyramids to protect their tombs, or hewing deep tunnels in the side of the cliffs that their bodies might be preserved to a life beyond death, do but illustrate, each in his own way, a fact so nearly universal that for our present purpose it matters little, if at all, that there may be some utterly savage groups, completely destitute of any such faith.

And now the question arises, how did men get that faith? Here again I shall not be appalled if I am told that in many lands the origin of this belief is associated with gross superstition; it could hardly be otherwise. I am familiar with the teachings of learned men as to how modesty, chastity, monogamy, law, order and morality arose from the dust and bore flowers. For faith in life beyond death I should not expect a much higher origin than can be traced for other doctrines which belong to a slowly developed civilization.

What concerns and profoundly impresses me is, that in a world where death is universal, a belief in life after death is almost, if not quite, universal also. That fact, whatever its explanation, is one of profound significance. Indeed, I shall go further, and shall say that *faith in immortality is even more astonishing than the fact of immortality.*

Let me illustrate that statement. Suppose I had

power to transform a frog into a bird, and wished to prepare the frog in some degree for what I was about to do. It is easy to imagine how I could perform the transformation, granted I had the power which the illustration assumes; but how could I possibly make the frog understand, being a frog?

Is the illustration grotesque? Let it be so, if it makes clear my meaning. It is much easier for me to imagine myself touching a frog with a wand and telling him to fly, and seeing him rise on newly created wings, than it is to conceive of any method by which I could educate him in froghood for the high privileges of birdhood.

Now if there be a wise and good and Almighty Father in Heaven, it is certainly possible for Him to grant eternal life to his children; but how can it have been possible for Him ever to have given to them the faintest glimmering of such a future? It seems so utterly inconceivable that one is tempted to declare it impossible. But just before we do this, we encounter the fact that men very generally, and in all conditions of society and civilization, have received in some way, an intimation of immortality.

The fact, if it be a fact, that God has eternal life in store for his children, is less wonderful than their faith in it. And I have some inclination to believe that the faith is evidence of the fact.

CHAPTER IV

THE QUEST OF TRUTH

THERE have been, and doubtless still are, some men too honest to admit a belief in immortality. We may recall the letter of Thomas H. Huxley to Charles Kingsley when the latter had written to comfort the great scientist in a time of deep sorrow. Huxley appreciated the well-meant endeavor, but answered that he could not arbitrarily divide his mind, giving one part of it steadfastly to scientific pursuits and the other to the indulgence of a hope for which he could find no scientific evidence. We can and must respect that spirit. Here is a man who needs comfort, and denies himself because he will not accept it at the sacrifice of truth. I have known such men, and I have honored them even while I have deplored what seemed to me a deficiency in their spiritual development. Let it be granted that now the hope for immortality is

41

greater than the actual belief in immortality. That is what might be expected.

> A man's reach should exceed his grasp,
> Or what's heaven for?

If any man shall say that faith in immortality is too stupendous for his acceptance, I will not condemn him. I wonder that there are not more such men. The fact of death is so ineluctable, and faith in immortality seems so out of character with conditions of life as we have them. I observe with great interest that St. Paul did not denounce men who lack such faith, nor call for their expulsion as heretics. In writing to the Corinthians he demanded that the church in Corinth should expel from its membership an immoral member; in dealing with other members who lacked faith in the life to come, he made no such suggestion. But he was not content that those who doubted so precious a truth should be left in their doubt. Lovingly, patiently and without reproof, he set himself to the task of showing to those whom he addressed that the hope of immortal life is reasonable, and that he who denies himself this comfort and inspi-

42

ration deserves, not denunciation as a heretic, but friendly guidance and instruction.

Certain thinkers, or men who suppose themselves to be thinkers, have prided themselves on such proof as they were able to adduce that man is a body and possessed of no soul. Professor Momerie well said of such:

"In the whole history of thought there are no grosser instances of slipshod reasoning and patent fallacies than those in which so-called 'exact thinkers' have sought to rid us of our souls."

I have a bit of sedimentary rock from a very low and ancient bed, and in it the fossil of a trilobite. The trilobites were abundant when there was not a backbone on earth. We find their fossils in the Cambrian rocks, and less abundantly up to the Carboniferous. The man who could find a living trilobite would get his name into many scientific books; but the trilobite itself would be good for nothing. Nature has forgotten that experiment. Yet there was a time when the earth and the fulness thereof was the trilobite's, and it seemed that all that could be necessary was for trilobites to grow larger and thicken their shells, that no other

43

form of life would ever rule the earth. But one day there appeared some courageous type that said, "I will risk the damage to my outer and unprotected self and use the material of the outer shell for a backbone within." It was a perilous thing to do; but Nature rather admired the audacity of the undertaking and ran a quivering thread of nerve along the bone, and made a little knob of nerve at its upper end; and the backboned creature began gradully to use the bunch of nerve instead of a shell, and the nerve became a brain. This was Nature's reward for the courage of the absence of the shell. And thenceforth the world was given over to the dominance of the creature without shell, but with a stiff spine and a brain. And Nature's exploration in the direction of the trilobite proved a blind alley.

So interested did Nature become in the creature with the backbone, she gave him large attention; and, indeed, there are few things more interesting to this day than backbone. Nature then began making coal for coming life possessing brains and backbones. And there the trilobite fossils cease. So far as we can see, the progress of the trilobite

44

ended without permanent advance along that line toward a dominant type of life.

The trilobite escaped some perils by remaining a trilobite, but the end of that choice was death. The creature that made the perilous choice of a spine chose the immediate hazard, but the final way of life.

Some one has written most interestingly of the moment of supreme peril in the life of the mosquito. It is when, having passed through several changes to adapt its life to the water in which it is born, it leaves the water behind. It finds itself possessed of wings and an instinct to use them, and makes its way out of the water. It has never been on land, and no mosquito has returned from the shore to assure its companions in the water-world. Its wings are wet and untried; there is no one to teach it how to use them; there is no one to help it up the bank; it faces a most appalling peril, one fatal to millions of mosquitoes. But all the mosquitoes that survive are those who make the venture.

Now that is an analogy for faith. For here I am, an inhabitant of the world in which I was born, feeling wings that have never been spread, and impelled by an inward impulse toward a life which faith alone reveals, and I make that venture of faith. I dare declare myself a child of the God I have never seen, and a citizen of the heaven where I have never been. I choose to climb the banks and leave the lower level for that of faith. The choice is not without its perils, but it is that which gives my soul companionship with God. It is the mightiest moment in the evolution of the soul—the moment in which it accepts its high-born destiny by an act of faith in the unseen. Some men have faltered and fallen back, but the career of those who have succeeded is the history of the spiritual progress of the human race.

There is no known process by which the soul can reach its spiritual heritage by passivity. We may not sit idly and await our transformation into the divine image by processes external to ourselves. If we are saved into our spiritual heritage it will be because God has appointed us heirs of salvation, and ordained the means for our evolution into the liberty of the glory of the children of God; and because we respond to the act of God by a mighty

46

effort of faith by which we apprehend and appropriate our divine heritage.

The earlier theories of evolution assumed that the progress of the world was by exceedingly slow and painfully laborious process. This is still partly true; but the advancement of life is also by opportune and decisive leaps and bounds. There are sudden and immediate transitions by which a form of life rises instantaneously to claim a higher sphere as its own. The experience of the mosquito is repeated in varying forms in the metamorphosis of other types; and it is analogous to spiritual transformation in which faith faces its problems and its privileges. The evolution of the human soul is an appeal to faith in an unseen God, a hazardous pilgrimage toward an unrealized destiny. All about us are the evidences of our relations with the world of matter, but within us is the impulse of the indwelling God who made us in his own image. The triumph of faith in human life, causing men to assert their divine heritage, is the supreme fact in evolution, and is analogous to a thousand facts which have marked the progress of life from its beginnings. It is the triumph of "resident force" over an environment of the material. It is the determination of the being made in the image of God to declare himself related not alone to the dust but also and supremely to the Deity.

There is no adventure so thrilling and hazardous as that of the soul in its quest of truth. The quest lies along no royal highway, straight and plain; it lies through regions as trackless as the path to the poles, and marked with the tragedies of men who have become confused, lost their way, and died in the wilderness. It is almost a wonder that mankind has not agreed to write "No Thoroughfare" at the beginning, and give up the quest. It would seem so much easier to take the world at its face value, its present cash value, and cease bothering about the meaning of things. But the soul of man rises to the challenge of the universe, and goes forth to find the meaning of things, and at the heart of that meaning he has good right to hope that he may find an eternal goodness.

It is not an easy quest. Do not deceive yourself on that point.

Men are incurably religious. They will still make the perilous adventure of faith. They will

48

send forth their souls into regions dark and fear-haunted, where there are no sure marks to guide them, and they will not come back, but will press on with ardor and glad heroism, determined to find a reason at the bottom of things, and that reason rooted in eternal goodness.

But the land through which they have to travel is not wholly a wilderness. There are wells here and there in the desert, and there is manna. Here and there is a landmark erected by a brave soul who has made some satisfying discovery; and on one high peak, where it catches the first light of dawn and holds it longest into the gloom, stands the Cross of Christ, and the light that illumines it streams from an empty tomb.

If our faith in immortality were really false, we should wish to know it. The sooner we get down to rock bottom the better. If the world is hopelessly bad, let us face the fact. If Pontius Pilate represents the last word in civil government, and Annas and Caiaphas are the real typical priests, and the voice of the people is not the voice of God, but the yell of the mob crying "Crucify Him!" let us know it. If death ends all, and even the Holy

49

One of God still sleeps in Joseph's tomb "in the lorn Syrian town," let us not delude ourselves with any false hopes. We can know the hard truth better than we can afford to hug a delusion.

But if these hopes are false hopes, what hopes are true? What hopes have better right to be true than these? What may more fittingly declare the justice of God and the sure reign of righteousness than this?

We are mistaken about so many things related to the making and government of the world, it is well for us not to be too dogmatic concerning matters on which we merely speculate; but it is a significant fact that our faith in immortality is bound up with our belief in the divine benevolence. The hope of immortality where it exists is inseparably bound up with the faith that goodness is at the heart of things. It is our faith in goodness that gives us faith in immortality. It is that same goodness that alone could make immortality worth having. We dare not affirm that life would be a failure if it had no continuance beyond the grave, but we are fully justified in declaring that life after death is a precious corollary of our faith in the goodness of God and of the value of life.

Life might be good, and not continue forever. God might be good, and have larger plans than that any one man should live eternally. But our hopes of life after death are inseparably related to our faith that God is good. Men will not believe in immortality, and in the face of the contradictions of life can not well believe in immortality, unless they first believe in the goodness of God. Not only so, but immortality on any other hypothesis would be not a blessing but a curse. If God be not good, we dare not risk another life if we can avoid it. And if God is good, it is not easy for us to imagine how that goodness can be compatible with the wasteful and reckless destruction of that which has cost Him most and has in it largest possibilities of worth to Him. Goodness and immortality stand or fall together. And they stand.

The blossom is not censurable for not being fruit; yet it would be a rash blossom that would deny its own capacity of growth into fruit. The worm is not at fault for not being a butterfly, but the worm is justly censurable if it denies itself whatever luxury and nobility of spirit may be possible to it in the contemplation and hope of being a butterfly some time. Whether any such prophetic premonition can come to a worm, we may not know. If into the mean little soul of the worm there can enter now any suggestion of what it is to be, the most foolish and utterly stupid thing the worm can do is to deny itself the assurance that one day it shall take to itself a form of beauty and the power of flight. We can imagine it a mirth-provoking experience for the worm to proclaim such an astounding faith. All the testimony of the senses would be present to deny it. The owl in his wisdom might well be expected to hoot at it, and every atheistic goose to greet its proclamation with hissing contempt. There would be no worm present to testify that it had ever seen a worm evolve into a butterfly. Yet if the worm with the aspiring soul were a truly wise worm it would trust its intuitions, its inspirations, its faith. It would say, "I intend to be just as good a worm as a worm can be, but I am more than a worm; I possess the promise and potency of becoming a butterfly. Nay, even now, in my soul, I am a butterfly."

We know another thing, that the worm that denies to itself the validity of this impulse of immortality is forever and hopelessly lost. That is to say, the worm that refuses to enter the chrysalis gets killed by the frost. The worm that thinks it not worth while to bury itself in a dark little place of its own spinning, but to live on in its wormhood, remains forever a creature of the dust, a thing to be trodden on and finally to perish in the cold. It is his trust in this which may be called his instinct of immortality that preserves his life at all, and preserves it to the coming glory of his later and more beautiful existence.

But there is still a further thought: The worm that hath this hope in him is not wholly a worm. You can not justify yourself in any scientific classification which disregards the fact that this prophetic hope establishes his genus among butterflies. It is not simply that he is to become a butterfly; even now, while he crawls, every scientist on earth will agree to his classification among the forms of life that have in them inherent capacity for flight. That is to say, we may affirm that any worm that hath this hope in him hath butterfly life. We may use, and the Bible does use, the present tense. It does not say "shall have," but "hath." There is no

53

mistaking the emphasis upon the present tense. It is strictly accurate and scientific. The instinct that is to drive the worm into the chrysalis must be reckoned with in a scientific study of the worm, and it compels his classification with the winged and beautiful forms of life. He that believeth hath the glorified life.

Let us make it as plain to ourselves as we can that this prophetic instinct in the worm that impels it to weave and enter the chrysalis does more than relieve the monotony of wormhood with a pleasant illusion of something that the worm does not know very much about. It is the thing that makes continuous and glorified life attainable, and it already makes the worm necessarily classifiable as something above a worm. It would be the most irrational thing possible for a worm to deny the authority and validity of that dim but potent hope. And if that would be folly for the worm, how much more so for us! By the grace of God, we are not worms. We are more than creatures that grovel in dust. And one of the things that make us so is the compelling power of this hope.

The hopes that elevate us above the dust, that

54

lift up our heads and give wings to our most ennobling and God-like aspirations, these are the hopes
which we have good right to possess. We need not
be too economical of them. They are a valid part
of the equipment which we bring to our quest of
truth.

CHAPTER V

A RIGHTEOUS GOD

BELIEF in immortality has for its inevitable basis some such foundation stones as these:

This world is to be interpreted as intention. It is the product of intelligence and conscious purpose.

The universe is friendly. There is in it a Power that possesses the quality of love. Love makes the mother bird capable of risking her life for her nest; love inspires the music and the blossom; love is at the core of things.

There is behind the phenomena of nature, and operative through nature, including the nature of humanity, a Power which is parental and personal. There is a mighty and a righteous God who cares what happens to his creation, and is great enough to accomplish what He knows to be best.

I find no rational basis for faith in immortality in any form of atheism. Unless there is a God who

56

loves, and has taught us to love; unless there is a God who possesses life, and has given us life, then I think faith in immortality is probably a delusion. As a matter of fact, I think people do not believe in immortality unless they believe in God. We must believe in a God who is strong enough to accomplish his will, else we shall sigh with Tennyson's King Arthur:

> O me! for why is all around us here
> As if some lesser god had made the world
> But had not force to shape it as he would?

And we must believe in a God with goodness equal to his power. We can not be happy in the contemplation of a God who is driving a pitiless Juggernaut over the suffering generations, working out a majestic program in which love has no part. Tennyson grew furious when he contemplated this possibility:

> No more! A monster then, a dream,
> A discord; dragons of the prime,
> That tear each other in their slime,
> Were mellow music matched with Him!

Thomas Hardy has considered the possibility that mortal man may be more just than his Maker;

that the creature may have evolved above the moral level of the being who created him; that man may have higher moral views of God than God himself possesses:

> Strange that ephemeral creatures who
>   By my own ordering are,
> Should see the shortness of my view,
> Use ethic tests I never knew,
>   Or made provision for!

Yes, that would be strange, so strange that we have little occasion to consider its possibility.

It is hardly conceivable that God would make creatures so much better than Himself that their perfection would mock his imperfection. It is not worth much time arguing that an immoral God would create morality, or that a God not Himself immortal would or could have bequeathed as a legacy which He never had, the gift of immortality to man.

There is no blackboard demonstration of the goodness of God; one must accept it on faith or die a coward. There is no way of making the matter perfectly sure. A man must be one

> Who trusts that God is love indeed,
> And love creation's final law,

Though nature red in tooth and claw
With ravin shrieks against the creed.

If he is not willing to risk that venture of faith, he will hardly arrive at a belief in immortality. Those who are without God are without hope in the world.

But let no man affirm too soon that he does not believe in God. Some men say they do not believe when they mean that they are bewildered or that they are seeking for more light. Let no such man call himself an atheist, for he is not.

There is one wide department in theological science called Teleology, which means reasoning from adaptation to creative purpose. It is an argument which, standing in the midst of creative energy, reasons forward with the good which is operative in the world to its logical result, and backward to the inferred intent of the Creator of that good. It assumes that agencies converging to a definite and rational result are the manifestation of intelligent purpose. There are forms of the teleological argument which are obsolete because they attempted too much. But the major premise of the teleological argument is sound, namely that order implies purpose; and the minor premise is the working principle of science, that the methods of the universe are orderly and rational and consistent.

I have a portrait of the President of the United States, woven in silk. I have seen the looms at work weaving patterns of this character. They are amazingly intricate, dropping a strip of perforated cardboard for each thread carried by the shuttle, and compelling fascinated attention by their bewildering ingenuity. The pattern is woven wrong side out, and the nature of the pattern is not always evident to the unskilled visitor. But any guess as to the pattern being woven is also a guess at the intent of the maker of the machine. That is the important point just now; the one end involves the other. We stand midway of the process, watching the mechanism of life. And when we learn a little of the end of life we have learned something also of the purpose of the God from whom life proceeds; and when we have learned something of the character of God we have some knowledge of the end toward which God works.

As I watch the loom, I may be confused and wonder whether the intelligence is in the machine or the maker or the operator. But in time I shall come to some definite opinion. The maker has wrought his own intelligence into the machine, and imparted a knowledge of his purpose to the operator; and so the maker, the weaver, and the machine conspire to a common and a definite end, an end which I may see if I am patient, and which in the case of my illustration, is the portrait of the President.

Life is such a machine, and I am myself the weaver as well as the journeying inquirer. And the answer to my puzzled inquiries is that life is working out a picture, a fabric, a product, an end. I see it wrong side out and I see it in the making; but there is the pattern, not stamped upon life with some foreign substance, but woven of the very stuff of human life. And I become assured that it is weaving out of the warp and woof of common manhood a transcript of the character of God as seen in the face of Jesus Christ, and reproduced in the lives of humble men and women. That is enough; and I may go on, like Oriental workers in silk, spinning as I walk; for I know the end for which it is designed.

61

In the Centennial Exposition in Philadelphia a little company gathered about a man who took from his vest-pocket a little box whose cover was a silver three-cent piece, and which contained a miniature steam engine. Its base was a gold half-dollar, and its boiler contained a dozen drops of water, more or less; but he lighted the tiny alcohol lamp, the water boiled, and the microscopic engine worked. He set it down on the base of the great Corliss engine that operated all the machinery of the Exposition, and the two ran side by side. The machinery of man is too clumsy for such an engine to share with the great Corliss the labor of operating the Exposition. But with God it is not so. It is permitted me to run a tiny thread to the great band-wheel of the universe, and yoke my energy with God's. It is not much, to be sure; and the few drops of alcohol in my lamp are burning fast; but I am not merely a part of the machinery that is being run; I am a part of the power that operates and controls. This is the end for which life was made. This is a part of the structural plan of the universe. This is the destination toward which we journey.

There is in the life of man a kinship with that of God which enables the mind of man to discern the purpose of God, and in that purpose to know the end. This is the needle of human certainty that points unerringly toward the pole of God's own intent. We can follow the needle when we can not see the stars. The road whose end is unseen is not an endless road. We walk by faith, not by sight, but we are not lost. We sail by "dead reckoning," but we are not derelict. We make our journey with inward assurance that we are following to the right end.

A visitor with no particular mechanical genius or interest, wandering listlessly and wearily through a great building in a World's Fair Exposition, will be likely to stand for a moment or two and regard with interest some particularly huge and complicated mechanism into which disappears a considerable quantity of raw material, as cotton thread or white paper, but of which no more is seen than that these things are swallowed up amid the clatter and whirr of the machinery. It will be the good fortune of some of these people as they pass along beside the great invention to see the finished product come out in woven cloth or imprinted newspapers. In that moment the observer has a momentary thrill like that of a discoverer, and says, "Why, it is weaving cloth," or "It is printing paper!" but the man in charge if he overhears, can hardly answer otherwise than, "Of course it is: that is exactly what it was made for."

The world is a mighty press or loom into which goes the raw material of life, and concerning whose processes and results there is more or less bewilderment and uncertainty. There is a current phrase which speaks of it, or of one man's part in it, as "the grind," and so mechanical is the thought of the age that the term is not without its appropriateness. But it has been given to some fine souls to discern the meaning of life's mechanism in its finished product, and they find this meaning so large, so exalted, that they can not restrain the discoverer's shout of "Eureka!" It is to these men that St. Paul addresses the confidant affirmation of the truth: "Now He that wrought us for this very thing is God." Have you discovered that man has before him a high destiny? St. Paul answers that it could not be otherwise. God hath wrought us, he

64

declares, for a mighty and triumphant purpose; a purpose disclosed in our present possession of the Spirit of God, by whom the work now in progress is to become complete. Hear these exalted words of his concerning the Godlike character to which we are ordained, and the glorious immortality to which we are bidden to aspire. "Now he that hath wrought us for the selfsame thing is God, who also hath given unto us the earnest of the Spirit."

The glory of the series of world's fairs which has erected one "white city" after another in various parts of our country has not caused some of us to forget the old exposition which annually for a series of years took place in Chicago. There I first heard Theodore Thomas in the old exposition building many years ago.

One day there came a village pastor to see the great exposition in Chicago, in its then new building on the lake front; and having a bent for mechanics, and some experience and skill, he soon sought the machinery; and, wondering that machines so many and varied should be running with power from a single source, he found his way to the engine room.

And what do you think he said when he saw the great engine?

He said, "I made it!" No; he was not insane, or deceiving. And the discovery was as complete a surprise to him as to those who heard him.

He examined the massive giant from end to end; there was no doubt about it; it was his very own. He had crept through its bulky boilers before they had a single flue; he had crawled beneath them when they were first set up; he had witnessed and superintended the casting of every part; he had overseen the adjustment of every bolt and valve and rod; it was his own!

As a boy he had been bred a mechanic, and had become a skilled machinist in a New England machine-shop. His firm established a branch house at Buffalo, and put him in charge of it. The greatest single work of the branch under his administration was the building of a powerful engine for the Adams mill on North Clark Street in Chicago. Trusted with the responsibility of so important a work, he spared no effort to do it superbly well; and when the engine was ready to be set up he came to Chicago and built the engine into its place.

In time he took a course in theology and entered the ministry, and became a pastor in Illinois. The Chicago fire had laid the city low, and the large mill had been destroyed; that chapter of his experience seemed to have left no memorial; it was, except to himself, as if it had not been. But when the debris of the fire had been cleared away, the fine engine was found but little injured. And so when George Huntington, then pastor of the First Church in Oak Park, visited the exposition, he found his own engine which he supposed perished; found it still strong and steady, and doing a bewildering variety of work far beyond the dreams of the man who made it.

After the road of life comes to what seems to us its abrupt termination; after the wreck and disaster of what we call death; the motive power of our present life will abide, indestructible. And I think we shall stand in heaven bewildered with wondering joy when we discover that the structure of life's mechanism is adapted to almost infinitely varied and celestial uses. We shall say with Paul, "Now he that wrought us for this very thing is God."

CHAPTER VI

THE DUST OF THE EARTH

WE ARE made of the dust of the earth. We know the chemical ingredients. We daily replenish by our eating the dust which we as constantly wear away. We are told, and I presume it is true, that so rapid is the attrition of this dust within us that as often as once in seven years an entire change takes place, and that no human being has in his body a particle of blood or bone or fiber which helped to compose his body seven years ago. To dust we shall return. We shall not be long about it. I have had but little experience in the removal of bodies once interred, but I have seen enough of it to know that a very few years suffice to leave of any man very little dust that can be distinguished as having ever belonged to him.

Moreover, the processes of our birth and development, the means of sustaining life and of its reproduction, all deal with facts so elemental, so close akin to the soil and smut that there is very little opportunity for any one to think of himself in terms of too great exultation. But if He who made us of the dust is God, then the very dust takes on new significance in that fact.

I dined one night with Professor T. C. Chamberlin of the University of Chicago, and I asked him, "What is the dividing line between Geology and Astronomy?" If I had been just a little more ignorant than I am, I might have supposed that the business of the geologist stopped with the surface of the earth; but I knew better than that.

He did not hesitate a minute. He knew just how far his science had property rights. He said that it ended at the point where the earth's attraction equaled that of the sun; the point on the one side of which a body would fall to the earth and on the other side toward the sun. He said that point, which varied more or less with the three unequal axes of the "spheres of control," had a minimum radius of 620,000 miles.

I asked, "That is all settled, is it?"

He said, "The precise distance in miles varies,

but the point when the earth's attraction equals that of the sun is the line of division between the astronomers and the geologists."

Now, the geologist deals with a science that is of the earth, earthy and of the rocks, rocky. His business is strictly underfoot. And yet when you tell him to keep his feet on the earth, here he is demanding 620,000 miles up in the air as belonging also to his science.

If the geologist whose science sends him around with a hammer knocking off pieces of rock demands 620,000 miles of room above his head for his science, I shall not heed for a minute the advice of those who admonish me to keep always on the level of the ground. I will not saw off my vision on the level of my eyes, or reserve just room enough to wear a silk hat without bumping into impractical theories. I am a child of earth, but I am also a child of God. The science with which I deal requires as its very base line all that the geologist counts his own; and if I get as much as that, I think I shall claim more. For all worlds belong to God; and if God is my Father, what is God's, is mine.

I also know about another line, that between

earth and sky. That line is not some hundreds of miles up in the air; it is the level of the ground. I walk and move in the sky. My feet are on the ground, but my head is not on the earth. When I swim in the little lake under my windows I have my body in one element and my head in another. So when I walk, my feet are on the ground, but the region where my head is, is as truly sky as is the space between the stars in the cluster of the Pleiades.

A few years ago there appeared in the newspapers a poem by James Oppenheim entitled *Earth's Song*. It is not in any sense a religious poem. It is a strong appeal based on the very substance of things in Mother Earth that have entered into the life of man, to rise above dust and be the crowning wonder of creation. In it the old earth remembers her girlhood, when warm and young she felt the love-warmth of the sun and thrilled with the pain and joy of motherhood, longing all the while to be

A planet disclosing to skies my glorious ones,
A world that should lead all the worlds, all the
    planets and suns;

and how she put more and more of her life and hope into each successive form of life to which she gave being, weeping over some of the pitiful dumb animals that as yet were her only children:

And I aged with despairing ages, till strange chil-
    dren walked
On the radiant hills, and in strange ways they
    talked.
My poor, dim children! Then with my might of
    mights,
Caught in birth-throes, caught in a fire of the
    heights
Of creation, I strained through that life to my top-
    most span,
And lo, on my breast lay my one sheer miracle—
    Man!

How the Earth-Mother gloried in that child of her old age—that miracle of maternity! How for the first time she felt on her bosom a child that could really know and understand and aspire!

Man that could answer me back from the hush
    where I dwelt,
Man that could think in his brain all the passion I
    felt,
Man that could light all my peaks with his laughter
    and song,
Man that could live and could love and could
    dream and could long.

72

How much of the stuff of earth and sky had gone into the making of this man!

O man, if you could but know what a glory you
     are!
Into you went the fire of the sun, my star;
Into you went the millions of ages of me!
Into you went the millions of ages to be!

How shall we answer the yearning of the ages for the expression of their finest aspirations and deepest longings in a manhood and womanhood that can know and feel and love as we are capable of knowing and feeling and loving!

We are made of the stuff of the glorious earth and the beautiful sky. We are children of star dust and sunlight. Into our being has gone the material of the stars and suns.

Aye, more than this, we are children of parental love from the beginning of time. Into our miraculous lives God has put the yearnings and patience and suffering hope of the ages. Into our lives have gone the prophetic smiles of mothers, and the honest toil of strong fathers since the first man and woman walked the earth. There is not a generation that has lived on earth since Adam was created to whom we are not debtors. Shall we repay this investment in our lives with only such return as men found possible in less favored ages? Shall we even be content to fall somewhat below their heroic and strenuous endeavor?

We are children of God. Into our lives has gone the sacrificial love of our heavenly Father, and the redemptive ministry of Christ. We have inherited the travail of the ages. With more of meaning than Napoleon before the battle of the Pyramids we may cry aloud to our souls, "A thousand centuries look down upon us."

We are made of the dust. That is good material. My friend, Professor Frost, of the Yerkes Observatory, explained to me the mysteries of the spectrum as the astronomer is able to isolate the light of a single star, and to determine accurately just what elements there are in process of combustion. He told me, as we stood beside the massive telescope, that this universe is really a universe; that the same essential elements, carbon, hydrogen, oxygen and the rest, which are the basis of our solar system, are the material bases of all the suns which his great telescope, pointing its long interrogation-point night by night out among the stars, can discover. He added that most of these same elements are in our own bodies; we are made of the best stuff in the universe.

That is a fine discovery. We thrill with all the fire of all the suns. We are akin to the dust and to the Deity. Angela Morgan has expressed this in one of her uplifting poems:

I am aware,
As I go commonly sweeping the stair,
Doing my part in the every-day care—
Human and simple my lot and share—
I am aware of a marvelous thing:
Voices that murmur and ethers that ring
In the far stellar spaces where cherubim sing.
I am aware of the passion that pours
Down the channels of fire through Infinity's
        doors:
Forces terrific with melody shod,
Music that mates with the pulses of God.
I am aware of the glory that runs
From the core of myself to the core of the suns,
        Bound to the stars by invisible chains,
        Blaze of eternity now in my veins,
        Seeing the rush of ethereal rains
Here, in the midst of the every-day air—
        I am aware.

MY FAITH IN IMMORTALITY

I am aware,
As I sit quietly here in my chair,
Sewing, or reading, or braiding my hair—
Human and simple my lot and my share—
    I am aware of the systems that swing
    Through the aisles of creation on heavenly
       wing;
    I am aware of a marvelous thing—
Trail of the comets in furious flight,
Thunders of beauty that shelter the night,
    Terrible triumph of pageants that march
    To the trumpets of time through Eternity's
      arch.
I am aware of the splendor that ties
All the things of the earth with the things of the
    skies,
    Here in my body the heavenly heat,
    Here in my flesh the melodious beat
    Of the planets that circle Divinity's feet.
As I sit silently here in my chair,
      I am aware.

CHAPTER VII

THE POWER OF LIFE

I SHOULD like to begin this chapter with an accurate definition of life. That would go far toward making the book immortal, for I do not know any dictionary which contains such a definition. When a learned lexicographer defines life as "the sum of those forces which resist death," he is simply saying that he does not know how to define life except in terms of its apparent opposite. And when he comes to define that opposite, he would have to return and say of death that it is that which opposes life. And so we should find ourselves midway between the two, with no definition of either. But we know what life is, even if we can not define it, and, as we are to consider the power of life, it would be well if we could define the word power.

Not only is it difficult to define the word, "power," it is not easy even to define the idea with entire clarity. The *Century Dictionary* devotes some three columns of closely printed matter to the attempt. It tells us that power is an endowment of a voluntary agent whereby it becomes possible for that being to do or effect something; or, a property of an inanimate thing whereby it is possible for it to modify other things. Negatively, and as the first definition, it is "such an absence of external restriction and limitation that it depends upon the inward determination of the subject whether it will or will not act." Very well; but, the external restriction being removed, what is it in the animate or inanimate object which causes the subject to act? What is power? What is gravitation, chemical affinity, electricity, sex-attraction, the ability of a maple tree to lift in the course of a season ten tons or a hundred tons of water, to say nothing of changing that water into sap and the sap into wood-fiber, leaf and blossom? The *Encyclopedia Britannica* has an interesting and intricate discussion on the transmission of power, but nothing about the nature of power itself. What is power? And in what sense is life, power?

Machinery does not produce power; on the contrary, it consumes power. The best locomotive wastes more than ninety per cent of the power that is resident in the coal. Machinery merely transmits or utilizes power. What is power itself?

This universe appears to be throbbing with power of several kinds. The kinds of power may be classified according to several categories; but viewed in one way there are two kinds, the kind that pulls and the kind that pushes. There is attraction and there is repulsion. Who knows what either of them is or why it operates? We know of some forces which are convertible into each other. We behold a flash of lightning, and define its energy as light. A tree is struck, and we discover the energy of lightning displayed as force. We place our hand on the wood that has been rent, and find it hot, and we learn that heat as well as light and force are potentially present in the lightning's flash. We may repeat the experiment with the electric wire in our room. It is possible to screw in a bulb that will give light, or the attachment of an electric iron that will develop heat, or the motor of a sewing-machine that consumes power. One kind of energy along the wire is thus convertible. In the chemical laboratory other transformations become possible.

But what of the controlling agent in all these experiments? Power is manifested which produces all these modes of energy, but there is no known way by which such energy can be produced by forces apart from antecedent energy.

Life itself is a power.

The question is hotly debated among physicists and biologists whether we are able to pass from the non-living to the living world without a break. There are eminent men who believe that, strictly speaking, all matter is alive. They hold that the laws of crystallization, and of atomic energy display agencies which are logically to be classified as living forces. If so, the universe is just so much more wonderful than we have supposed; nor are we at all disturbed by their discussions. We still wonder with John Burroughs at the power and persistency of life:

When for the third or fourth time during the spring or summer I take my hoe and go out and cut off the heads of the lusty burdocks that send out their broad leaves along the edge of my garden or lawn, I often ask myself, "What is this thing

80

that is so hard to scotch here in the grass?" I decapitate it time after time and yet it forthwith gets itself another head. We call it burdock, but what is burdock, and why does it not change into yellow dock, or into a cabbage? What is it that is so constant and so irrepressible, and before the summer is ended will be lying in wait here with its ten thousand little hooks to attach itself to every skirt or bushy tail or furry and woolly coat that comes along, in order to get free transportation to other lawns and gardens, to fresh woods and pastures new?

It is some living thing; but what is a living thing, and how does it differ from a mechanical and non-living thing? If I smash or overturn the sun-dial with my hoe, or break the hoe itself, these things stay smashed and broken, but the burdock mends itself, renews itself, and, if I do not watch out, will surreptitiously mature some of the burs before the season is passed.

Evidently a living thing is radically different from a mechanical thing; yet modern physical science tells me that the burdock is only another kind of machine, and manifests nothing but the activity of the mechanical and chemical principles that we see in operation all about us in dead matter; and that a little different mechanical arrangement of its ultimate atoms would turn it into a yellow dock or into a cabbage, into an oak or into a pine, into an ox or into a man.

Apart from all technical definitions with which

81

we have no quarrel, there is such a thing as vital force. A titled woman in Germany, having no faith in immortality, had the courage of her convictions, or the lack of them, and caused herself to be buried in a tomb of masonry covered with a heavy stone slab, on which was inscribed a declaration of her opinion that was the end for her. She was mistaken. A tiny seed found lodgment in the mortar, took root that fed upon her body and grew to a tree that burst the slab asunder. I have seen a photograph of the tree growing from this tomb proclaiming nature's own refutation that death is a finality or the tomb impregnable.

Just as surely as the tree has inherent in its life the power of lifting water and transforming it into sap and wood-fiber and leaf and blossom, so has the spiritual life its own lifting power. It can raise men out of despondency, desolation and sin. It can lift and transfer them and make them sons of God. It can give them a hope which is more than a gentle and pleasurable sensation; a hope that is alive and full of dynamic vigor.

It is a hope that is as certainly capable of transforming life as an alkali is of modifying an acid.

"Every man that hath this hope in him, purifieth himself, even as He is pure." It is a hope that makes life more worth living, and that robs death of its terror. It is the power of an endless life.

The lifting power of life is marvelous, whether manifest in the tree lifting tons of water, or in man lifting his own weight in walking; but the most significant fact about the power of life is not its ability to *lift* but its ability to *select* and *direct*. Doctor William Hayes Ward, toward the end of his long and fruitful life, published a book entitled, *What I Believe and Why*. In this he says:

It is of the very essence of life that it gives guidance, is purposive. This separates it from mere physical forces, such as the attraction of chemism. It has a previsioned end to achieve. It aims to create a man, a tree, then to keep them repairing themselves or growing to an ideal perfection. Out of the common sap the atoms distribute themselves after a preconceived scheme to organize into bark, wood, leaves, petals, stamens, pistils, seeds, just as we knew they would when we planted the peach stone. This is very purposeful life. Life chooses, sorts, selects, directs, sees and reaches a distant aim. Whence comes this outreaching, selective, directing power?

The mere biologist does not try to answer this

83

question. He is content to see it, to state its laws and give names to the usual processes of life, and then he too often thinks that the naming of a law is an explanation of its force. An apple falls to the ground. We ask "Why?" and we are told that the attraction of the earth draws it. *Attraction* is from the Latin word *attraho,* meaning to draw; and so we are told that *drawing* draws it and get nowhere. We have simply given a general name to a familiar fact, but why the apple falls to the earth, we have not learned. So vitalism, or vital force, is but a name we give to an observed order of process. It explains nothing. Its marked character is its foresight.

That interesting, provocative and depressing book, *The Education of Henry Adams,* has an illuminating chapter on "The Dynamo and the Virgin." It is a kind of foot-note to the author's effort to discover a dynamic theory of human history. What is the motive power of society? He says that he haunted the French Exposition of 1890, "aching to absorb knowledge and helpless to find it." In that same fruitless quest he had gone through Harvard, had studied law, had taught History, and apparently his education had made him increasingly ignorant. The sum total of ignorance which he accumulated during a life of study

84

was colossal. In this Exposition he became mightily interested in the dynamo, particularly in its application to the use, the beginning, of the automobile. He also learned about radium, which as he said, "denied its God," or what to a certain scientific friend of his was the same thing, "denied the truths of his science" in which all forms of energy were supposed to have been tabulated and defined. Neither in science nor in history was he able to discover a sequence between cause and effect, between the springs of human action and recorded fact. Certain superficial relations were apparent, but what and where was the power?

In the Exposition stood a notable work of American art, the General Sherman statue by Saint Gaudens, which now stands at the entrance of Central Park in New York. There was the lean, lithe, nervous, determined man; and under him was the thin, wiry, swift, capable horse that bore him "from Atlanta to the Sea"; and before this group was the female figure, a Winged Victory. "For a symbol of power, Saint Gaudens instinctively preferred the horse. Doubtless Sherman also preferred it. The attitude was so American that, for at least forty years, Adams had never realized that any other could be sound taste." Adams said that Saint Gaudens, who was with him in Paris, "could never discuss or dilate upon an emotion, or suggest artistic arguments for giving to his work the form which he felt." The two went to Amiens and looked at the Cathedral, and Adams reflected that that magnificent temple represented the triumph of a power beyond that which Sherman's horse could represent, and which Saint Gaudens felt but could not articulate, when he placed the symbolic figure in front of the swiftly moving steed. The worship of the Virgin built Amiens. Artists of this generation, even those like Saint Gaudens at Amiens, and Matthew Arnold at Chartres, "felt a railway train as power; yet they, and all other artists, constantly complained that the power embodied in a railway train could never be embodied in art. All the steam in the world could not build a cathedral. That called for worship, it might be superstitious worship, but it was worship expressive of a power above and beyond that of the dynamo.*

---

*The Education of Henry Adams, pp. 387-8.

The more intimate and closely reasoned studies of life which have characterized our time have compelled a new and more careful analysis of the phenomenon of death. And we make this discovery, that death and life are not complete opposites. We do not speak with entire accuracy when we say that a lifeless thing is "dead as a door-nail." A door-nail is not dead, for it has never lived. Death is not to be affirmed of a thing that has not had life. Death is itself a phenomenon of life, the final phenomenon, as it appears to the observer, but even so a less instantaneous and single matter than has been supposed. Life continues, so recent scientific tests affirm, in certain organs after the death of the body. Particular organs have been removed from a dead body, and have manifested the power of life for variable periods. Death is a thing to be predicated only of things that have lived; and of its totality and finality we can not afford to be dogmatic. We have much to learn.

It is not in its biological but in its ethical and spiritual aspect we are concerned with these matters of life and death. We deal with it as a universal experience with important spiritual implications.

Death is an event which every man must face as a certain experience of his own. It is the great leveler. It is like the flood of Noah's day; there is no man tall enough to rise above it.

For the vast majority of mankind, death has no especial significance. For very many it is a very stupid and commonplace event. They simply lie down and stop breathing. Some may be longer about it than others; some groan, some lie quiet; but all die.

But now and then there is a man who makes some death significant. He may do this in one way or in another. Abner died as the fool dieth. Others have died likewise. In that fashion they wrenched death from the commonplace and flung life away to the accompaniment of folly.

But other people have succeeded in dying nobly, immortally. It is not wholly the manner of their death. Jesus and the two robbers had an identical experience so far as the crucifixion went; but his cross was not like theirs. Somehow, Jesus was able to meet death in a way that robbed that great enemy of his victory. Jesus made death significant.

88

It is the glory of the soldier who fights for a great cause that he is able to utilize an experience which he must share with all sorts and conditions of men, and even with the brute creation, and make it significant.

Some men have said that if Jesus Christ had lived the life He lived and taught the truths He taught, and died a natural death, it would have meant as much to the world.

They talk nonsense.

If Jesus had lived as He lived, his life would have been unspeakably precious; if He had taught as He taught, the truths He uttered would have been among the greatest heritages of mankind; but his life and his teachings take on a dignity and spiritual significance *with his death* which the great teachers from the apostles down have rightly evaluated.

Death may be a very insignificant event.

It is easy to die; men have died for a wish or a
  whim;
 For bravado, passion or pride.

Yes, that is true. Some deaths have been inconsequential; some might as well have occurred years before they did, and the world would have been, if anything, better; some deaths have been wasteful, and some have been shameful; but some have been noble, and have inspired the lives of later generations as living alone could never have inspired them.

We hardly need to be reminded of the brevity of life.

It is the universal testimony of old men that to them life has seemed short. Even a life of three score years and ten is a restricted life, and if by reason of strength the years be four score, yet the life is soon cut off.

All of our plans are made with the knowledge that we may not live to carry them out. We press through the world with a feverish haste as if we were not to be here long.

The Apostle James, the brother of Jesus, asked, "For what is your life?" and answered: "It is even a vapor, that appeareth for a little time, and then vanisheth away."—James 4:14.

He was speaking well within bounds when he compared life to vapor. Measured in the proportion of its length to the boundless extent of time,

the life of any one man is too brief to be represented by a vapor; measured by the proportion of
his bulk to the mass of the universe he is altogether
too insubstantial and insignificant to be thought of
even as the tiniest speck in a vapor.

If the man of science be asked concerning human
life in its relation either to the stretch of time or the
bulk of the universe, he would say what James said
and say it more emphatically.

If we take a handful of marbles, one of them
large and glistening, the others small and varied in
size, and roll them around in a silk hat, we might
get a scale for the measurement of our solar system
in its relation to the rest of the universe.

Placing that solar system in Chicago, with our
world perhaps as a pea among the marbles, one
might start and walk to Cleveland one way and to
Omaha the other before he began to find many of
our nearer neighbors among the fixed stars, and
the world is not wide enough for us working upon
that scale of proportion to reach anywhere near the
edge of the visible universe in which our sun is a
mere speck of golden dust—one of the smaller
stars in the Milky Way.

91

In such a universe, what is a solar system like ours?

What is our world, and what is man?

Of man, in his relation to the universe, Harry Kemp has written:

God made a million atoms, each by mortals called
    a "world";
Like dust-motes in a beam of light, they dartled,
    circled, whirled;
Yet all these million worlds, compared to all his
    might did rule,
Were in the Universal Whole one tiny molecule.

The mortals on these shining specks spake of God's
    space as "far,"
And every bright companion-mote they hailed as
    "world" or "star."
(They should have known the Eternal Mind no
    need for measures hath;
God looketh down the Milky Way as down a gar-
    den path;
The distance from our outmost sun unto his
    throne, no doubt,
Is a hand's breadth in his seeing, or too small to
    measure out.)

These manikins then fought and died on many a
    shining mote—
For what they dubbed as "empires" sworded one
    another's throat;

Each nation on its anthill swarmed and sang a pa-
    triot song,
And stormed another anthill to avenge an emmet-
    wrong:
And thus they hated, loved and lived until the end
    of time,
While up the weary rounds of life a million worlds
    did climb.

Then flash! Two molecules collide and worlds ex-
    hale in mist,
And back into a fiery ring do melted empires twist,
And cities in solution hang and drop in fiery rain,
And the sinew of the tiger fuses with the poet's
    brain;
All back into one element trees, mountains, oceans,
    glide,
And not one life is left to strut and swell in pom-
    pous pride—

Then some far-worlded telescope which chance did
    thither turn
Beholds this starry funeral pyre minutely flame
    and burn.
"Lo!" thinks the awed astronomer, his star-map at
    his side,
"Upon yon utmost verge of night a star was born
    and died."
And so they numbered eons there, and cherished
    histories gray!
Oh, but they battled, loved and dreamed for a
    clock-tick in God's day!

Life is a vapor. But what is a vapor? It is all that it ever has been. It was a pearly raindrop that fell down from the skies; and as it fell, it brightened and made beautiful the flower in whose golden heart it lay, and then, dropping to the earth, watered the root that there might be other flowers; and then, by subterranean channels breaking forth into a spring, it flowed singing to the sea, turning the wheels of industry as it went, and laughing in the sunlight as it bore great ships upon its blue bosom.

The sun caught it up and it vanished into heaven, smiling as it rose. All this the vapor was and is; all this it did and does. It appeareth for a little while and then vanisheth away.

But when it vanishes it rises fragrant with the odor of the flowers it has refreshed, dignified by the burdens it has borne, radiant with the honor of thirst it has quenched, and jubilant in the memories of service it has rendered.

It vanishes away, but as it vanishes, the sun catches it up into heaven, pours through it the sevenfold glory of its prismatic splendor and imparts to it a radiance fit for the diadem of God.

94

It vanishes away, but as it vanishes it smiles in the glow of promise of joyful service still to be, and its rainbow gladdens the eyes of men and reminds them of the covenant of God.

There are lives like that. They appear for a little time and then vanish away. But they come to earth trailing clouds of glory, and they vanish fragrant with the memories of a beautiful and varied ministry to their fellow men.

They flow through the channel of their years, leave behind them holy and sacred memorials, and when they vanish they overarch the two worlds; at this end are glorious memories, and the gold at the other end of their rainbow is the pavement of the city of God.

And the vapor is not lost. It is one of the certainties of modern science that every particle of the vapor abides. It disappears, but it is indestructible. We see it:

> Like the snowdrop in the river,
> A moment white, then fades forever.

Forever? No! It has fallen, faded, risen and blessed the world a million times; and unborn generations will see it, taste it and be refreshed by it.

There are lives like that. They come to earth, live, love and pass away. But they are not lost. The sweet influences by which they made life better are added to the invisible cords that bind the world to the throne of God. They are not lost. They live, and live forever.

CHAPTER VIII

SCIENCE AND IMMORTALITY

IT IS often affirmed that science knows nothing of life after death. This is true. It is also true that it knows next to nothing about this present life. Science observes life as a phenomenon and is able to classify some inferences and deductions concerning it, but that does not imply that science understands the present life of man.

I have seen in a medical college a series of jars containing the constituent ingredients of a human body. There was a large glass vessel containing a few gallons of water; there was a smaller jar containing a few pounds of lime; and there were salts and solids of various sorts, a spoonful of iron and a pinch of phosphorus. It was an interesting exhibit and doubtless had its educational uses, but no student, I am confident, was ever encouraged to suppose that he would be taught in that school how to mix together that water and lime and the rest and make a man.

Furthermore, if scientists were not themselves men, and had never seen a man, and had only those jars of material at hand, they would have been as helpless to conjecture anything about this present life as they now are and must be about the life to come. Concerning this life, they are able to talk and write with a modest approach to wisdom, but they could not have imagined it if they had never seen it. But here it is, strange beyond all comprehension yet undeniably real. If their scientific investigation does not prove a future life, neither does it prove a present life, apart from the actual experience of it. No scientist claims more than this, and, if he can not prove a life after death, neither can he prove that such life does not exist.

Inertia is a property of matter; but growth is a law of life. Each lifeless thing in all this vast universe will stay where it is placed until something moves it, and remain as it is until something changes it; but every living thing though molded by forces without, is also shaped by powers within. The inorganic world is static; the organic world is progressive. Moved upon by the forces of vitality, dead matter feels within it the throb and thrill of life and responds to laws beyond its own domain. This is the perpetual miracle of nature. In the tree that lifts its tons of earth and water high in air, and transforms them into sap and leaf and fruit; in the flower that roots itself in unfeeling soil and turns it into petals of beauty and of grace; in the bird that eats matter and sings music; in the man who consumes carbon and oxygen and thinks thoughts that soar among the stars and explore the long reaches of eternity, the law is the same. In each and every one of them, life transforms matter by the laws not of matter but of life. Inertia gives way to growth; the laws that govern from without share their domain with forces resident within. In every one of them is wrought the change spoken of by the Apostle Paul: the corruptible clothes itself with the glory of the incorruptible; mortality is swallowed up of life. Matter ceases to be dead. Earth becomes "crammed with heaven, and every common bush afire with God." Inertia still is a law of matter; but life rules matter. Upon the inert forms of matter are stamped the impress of

99

animation; and within it are the potency and the passion and the progress that belong to life.

Gradually, and through a number of centuries, the thinking of the world has modified with respect to the relation of life to the universe. Changes that are recent go back in their beginnings and are seen to have been involved in discoveries much more remote.

In 1542 Copernicus published a book which he had completed twelve years before, but had withheld for fear of persecution, showing the sun and not the earth to be the center of the solar system. It was nearly a hundred years before that theory as enunciated by Galileo came to the attention of Pope Urban VIII, who demanded the recantation of Galileo. Galileo recanted, but the earth moved, and continued to move.

Meantime, other minds were moving with the earth. In 1687 Isaac Newton set forth his theory of gravitation, showing the invisible power that holds the planets in their orbits round a central sun.

Still another hundred years, and in 1796 La Place published his *Exposition du Système du Monde,* in which he set forth his Nebular Hypothesis. And even a little before his time James Hutton had uttered the first word of the new Geology, declaring the rocks to have been laid through successive ages which reveal "no trace of a beginning; no prospect of an end."

In 1858 Charles Darwin published his *Origin of Species,* and in 1871 his *Descent of Man.* It now appears that there was uninterrupted progress from the beginning of this series of movements. They begin with astronomy and end with man, even as the psalmist considered the heavens as the works of God's fingers and then bowed in wonder before the greater power that made man but little lower than God, and crowned him with glory and honor.

It would be safe to say that no one of these theories stands to-day precisely as enunciated by its author. Copernicus, Newton, Hutton, La Place and Darwin have all given place to later interpreters of the universe. Yet each of them wrought an epoch-making change in the thought of the world. We may discard the Copernican theory, but we never shall go back to the Ptolemaic. We may give up the theory of star-dust as held by La Place, but we shall never go back to a theory of instanta-

neous creation. We may think of Darwin as an
obsolete authority, but we shall never re-establish
the theories of life that existed before his day. The
changes which wait our thought in future lie not
behind us in the line of progress. Straight ahead
they may not lie, but backward they do not and can
not retreat. New theories may not have come to
stay, but the old ones have gone forever.

There is a very real sense in which religion is
independent of all these changes. God, sin, duty,
salvation, are all the same to men whether they live
on a flat earth or a round one; whether the earth
was created in a week or a million years, whether
man was originally perfect or has ascended from
lower life. No man ever had a right to nail the
truth of the Bible to the questionable truth of his
theory about the order of events in the first chapter
of Genesis. And those do still err, and greatly,
who assume that men have great spiritual need to
settle as spiritual concerns the doubtful and changing hypotheses of current science. The apostle
who said that neither circumcision availeth anything nor uncircumcision, would have said that, for
the real problems of the soul, neither evolution

102

availeth anything nor special creation, but faith that worketh by love; and that though we have all knowledge and understand all mysteries we shall have missed the real spirit of religion unless we have the spirit of Christ.

Yet because the religious thought of every age expresses itself in the language of that age; and because religion relates itself to the whole man, it has become inevitable that theology should have come to express itself in terms of more or less scientific analogy. If we are to have any books that perform for this generation such service as *Butler's Analogy* performed in its own age, those books must do what Butler did, must employ the latest words of science as it now is. If there is any *Natural Law in the Spiritual World,* that natural law must be interpreted in terms of modern science, and according to the analogies of the men whose business it is to know science. Hence, naturally, inevitably, and very properly, our religious writing has been cast in a scientific mold; and the evolutionary philosophy is in our religious treatises, and in our high school text-books, and in our college lecture rooms, and in our theological seminaries.

It is not incumbent on the modern minister that he preach evolution. It matters little to the content of his message how men came to be what and where they are. His message is to men as he finds them, and has respect to what they may become. But this is incumbent on any minister in any age, that he speak the language of his generation, and clothe his thought in the terms of his contemporaries. He may speak with the tongues of men and angels, but he will be to his own generation a barbarian unless he utters his message in the nomenclature of his own day. If he preach in a region where men believe the world flat, he need not assume it to be his duty constantly to proclaim the theory of a round earth, but he will be careful not to seem to make the flat earth a cardinal doctrine of religion. The shape of the earth does not greatly concern his message; but it is important that his message shall express itself in terms of the best knowledge of those to whom it is delivered.

Hence it has come about that all our present-day preaching and writing more or less assumes the phraseology of scientific speech; and even those who oppose the conclusions adopt the terms of the scientific world.

We have no need to decry this condition. We could not help it if we wanted to, and we do not want to do so. To try to keep it back would be Mrs. Partington's attempt to mop out the Atlantic. Upon the sea our boat is launched and we are in the boat.

But it is all the more important that we know how far and in what direction these theories bear us, and within what limits we have chart and rudder. For there are some who adopt the theories of progress in ascending life, who have not fully reckoned with their import. And there are others who assume that because the universe shows progress and plan, there is little need of anxiety or concern: for "God's in his heaven: all's right with the world."

But the doctrine of evolution, while a doctrine that strengthens our argument for an all-embracing purpose of an invincible God, is a very solemn doctrine as applied to the responsibility of the individual man. It offers no escape for unfaithfulness; it teaches no lesson of comfort to him who neglects his duty.

For a generation we have talked about the strug-

gle for existence and the survival of the fittest.
And sometimes we have spoken words of truth, and
again we have spoken words of cruel error. For
that which constitutes fitness for the struggle does
not always constitute fitness for the survival.
Some years ago Doctor Reuen Thomas uttered a
warning lest too shallow a view of evolution make
us cruel and unfeeling, and directed the mind of
those whom he addressed to its deeper and often
neglected lesson of brotherhood and the social
spirit as taught in nature:

For a generation we have been almost slaves to
two ideas which are associated with the name of the
great naturalist Darwin. One idea goes by the
name of "Natural Selection" and the other we
know as "the Survival of the Fittest." Natural Selection, of course, means that Nature favors some
organisms instead of others in consequence of dif-
ferences in the organisms themselves. The "fittest
to survive" are those which are most adaptable to
the surroundings in which they find themselves.
These two ideas have had the field and have
wrought most disastrously in politics and in the political use of military power. We have had to
listen to the horrible dogma that Nature intended
and therefore the Author of Nature intended that
the strong should subdue the weak. Small nations
were intended to be exploited by large nations.

"We that are strong ought to bear the infirmities of the weak, and not to please ourselves"—such apostolic words were laughed out of court. Militarism got a new sanction. The old George III Toryism lifted up its head in England once more. Nature was Tory. Brotherhood as an ideal and an aim was scouted.

Recently men have risen who, working along evolutionary lines, have pushed into mental and moral regions, and have shown that such ideas as those by which we have been enslaved, have a larger content than their originators perceived. The physically strongest may be only representatives of a gilded barbarism. The most effective among men (and even among animals) have been those capable of coming into fraternities for mutual helpfulness. There is, if only we will look for it, a Sermon on the Mount embedded in Nature. When once we have the fine tone and temper of that sermon in ourselves, we shall find it elsewhere. People are ruled by ideas. If our ideas of life and its purpose are wrong, our politics will be wrong, our domestic life will be wrong, all our conduct will be wrong in spirit and in tendency. To say "it does not matter what your opinions are providing your life be right" is arrant nonsense. The last note in evolution is that we are members one of another.

The theory of evolution does not assure us that all progress shall be upward. It assumes that life presses outward from its various centers in every direction, seeking unoccupied space for itself. It

107

often grows downward. The white ghost-flower called Indian pipe was once a true flower, with red petals, but growing in the shade it lost the glow from the blossom and the green pigment of the stalk; it now grows in the dark glen, hanging its head for shame, the ghost of its former self. It has made progress, and has found a place where it may survive. But its progress has been degeneracy, and the only place it now can live is in the dense shadow of other vegetation that has learned to nourish itself in the sun.

We do well to remember, and it is pleasant and profitable to remember, that the perishing of ancient Greece has left us, not the bickerings and petty commonplaces of her ordinary life, but those monuments to her greatness that stand out in bold relief above all that could degrade them by too intimate a knowledge of the meaner elements in the lives of the men who produced them. But we need also to remember how much good has escaped, and how much evil has survived as the years have gone by.

Nature has shown some of her most consummate skill in the fashioning of creatures for our torment.

What, for instance, is more perfectly adapted to its end than the proboscis of the mosquito? Some of the types least desirable have longest lease of life. Aristotle theorized about the origin of certain insect pests; Aristotle died, and his theory is obsolete, but the pests are with us still. The gnat and the flea harassed the armies of antiquity. Leonidas and his three hundred Spartans died at Thermopylæ and their descendants in Chicago peddle fruit from push-carts; but the insect scourges of the ancient world are still with us in unabated vigor.

The theory of evolution does not assure us that there shall be no failures; it does not promise that there shall be no loss of type, no experiment not visibly productive of good; but it gives us hope that creation as a whole shall not fail, and that the highest types will dominate.

The doctrine of evolution may be interpreted not as antagonistic to immortality, but as almost requiring it. It may cause us to look backward across the ages in which we have battled with a brute ancestry, and say with Paul, "If after the manner of men I have fought with beasts at

Ephesus, what advantageth it me, if the dead rise not?" It may cause us to declare with Tennyson that the very facts of our humble origin affirm that we were born to higher things than the life of the beasts that perish, and to an inheritance incorruptible, undefiled and that fadeth not away:

> I trust I have not wasted breath;
>   I think we are not wholly brain,
>   Magnetic mockeries; not in vain
> Like Paul with beasts I fought with death.
>
> Not only cunning casts in clay;
>   Let science prove we are, and then
>   What matters science unto men,
> At least to me? I would not stay.
>
> Let him, the wiser man who springs
>   Hereafter, up from childhood shape
>   His action, like the greater ape,
> But I was born to other things.

Any thinking person must now and then seek in his own mind an explanation of existing things. When we once have learned, as we soon must learn, that an effect implies a cause, we find ourselves seeking causes for all perceived effects. Not only so, but we seek to unify our knowledge, and to find a cause sufficiently great and inclusive to account for all existence. Our difficulty is not wholly one of bulk. If that were all we could mentally multiply the power of causation as we perceived the aggregate and diversity of effect. What troubles us is that we have so many kinds of effect and such apparently contradictory effects. If we were mind only and not matter, we might the more easily account for mind; or if we were matter only, and yet able to think at all, we might with the more consistency become materialists. But we still must say with Byron that "If Bishop Berkeley says there is no matter, then it is no matter what Bishop Berkeley says." And we say to the materialist that even such thinking as he does is a denial of materialism. Matter and mind are both here, and the two combined are more than twice as hard to account for as either one alone. Good and evil are both here. That fact would not be strange if there were two eternal and equally balanced principles, each represented by a god equal in power to his opposing god; but it is very difficult to account for if there is but one God. For most people it is convenient to divide the universe very nearly into

111

two equal parts and to hold the devil accountable for about half of what occurs.

If everything appeared to us to be good, it would not be difficult to hold the theory that all that exists is caused by one God and He a good one. But when we discover things that appear to us to be certainly evil, it is easier to think that there is one evil god, even though a minor one, who is responsible for that part of creation. To attribute the world to one infinitely good God is still more than all good people are willing to undertake.

It is this apparent dualism in the universe as we behold it, this alternation of light and darkness, this co-existence of matter and spirit with an undefined relation between them, this see-saw of joy and pain, this bringing forth of life to be swallowed up in death, this age-lasting struggle between good and evil, which we find so difficult to ascribe to the consistent operation of any one God, be He either good or evil.

Yet, while life's experiences might seem to imply two antagonistic forces, working forever at cross-purposes, science does not admit this dualistic system. We are not at liberty to assume that the wind

112

and the sun, or the cloud and the sun, are hostile each to the other, for the sun causes both cloud and wind. Forces that appear antagonistic work to a common result. The earth is held in its orbit by the balance of forces, not hostile but antithetic.

Thus, as science has thought its way back to a theory of essential unity, and in so doing walks by faith and not by sight, theology is constrained to exercise "like precious faith" and hold to the existence of one God, and He a good God.

The new sciences of the last generation have not failed to modify our thought of God. There have been at least a dozen of them. Comparative religion is new; comparative philosophy is new; comparative anatomy is new. Every science that uses the adjective "comparative" is new. Historic criticism is new; history itself is new. It is no longer a mere chronicle of events. It is a philosophy and interpretation of life in the perspective of these events. It is a study of cause and effect in the light of human happenings. Social science, sociology, is new. Every other science with the adjective "social" is new. All these sciences of life and all the physical sciences that use the microscope, that use electricity, that use radium, that use the X-ray, all are new. I well remember when I first looked through my hand with the X-ray. Every science that recognizes the penetrability of matter to light, and every science that attempts to make real the relationships of matter to force is new. Half the theories of yesterday are on their way to the scrap heap, and they have not left unmodified our conception of God. We are bound either to move God very much farther away or bring Him very much closer into the actual thick of the conflict of life. The conception of God just barely outside, the conception of Paley's Natural Philosophy, of a universe which God wound up like a watch and left for us to find, a universe initiated by a God who went off and forgot it, save for an occasional intrusion by the process of a miracle— that conception of God, good as it was in its day, will not answer for our present thinking. It is not adequate to the strain; God must be moved further away, or brought closer than in the thought of the old theology—and the old theology was good in its day.

Science is far from being the enemy of faith,

Doctor Edward A. Birge, who retired in 1925 from the presidency of the University of Wisconsin, devoted his last baccalaureate address to a confession of faith, as he had learned it simultaneously from Science and Religion.

The text of the address, if we may borrow a term from the sphere of homiletics, was the scripture:

"Whereunto shall we liken the Kingdom of God? or with what comparison shall we compare it? It is like a grain of mustard seed, which groweth up."

In early Greek philosophy, and now in modern science, Doctor Birge believed he saw the growth of the "eternal truth" to which each century adds a little and which each thinker serves in his own way. He is sure that the processes of the past, whose results are now apparent, are operative in the same way to-day and with the same certainty of continued advance.

Science had first assembled the facts of the world much at random and in helter-skelter fashion. Then it had gradually seen that they were integral parts of a structure. Later it was realized that the world was an operating affair, an organized and going concern, with its own methods and laws. Now there was added the full conception of a past and a future, of an historical development, of an evolution which could be read in the light given by present operations, just as the laws of the Kingdom of God may be found in the growth of the mustard seed.

With this idea as a clue, a new and limitless field was opened to science, a field which it has only begun to explore, whose extent is even yet unknown. But the short century since 1830 has seen advances into it along certain lines. For just as Lyell was completing his *Principles of Geology,* Darwin was beginning his studies on the species, and twenty-five years later he was to apply to that side of the problem of life the same fundamental principles that Lyell had applied to the history of the earth. Darwin told us that if we want to begin to know how species have come about, we must look first to the pigeon house, to the barnyard, to the grain field, and see what forces are operating there. Here are processes to be followed out; here is an evolution of forms, and the forces behind it are not those exercised suddenly by the intervention of unknown and incalculable energies; they are those now at work in the world about us. To this world as a present going concern we must look if we are to understand its past, knowing that out of the past the present has come. The kingdoms of life in all their multiform greatness are expressions of the same forces and laws that determine the growth of the mustard seed.

116

After nearly nineteen centuries of reading, the parable of the mustard seed is at last, through the aid of science, coming into its own.

Look where we may—consider universes or stars, or turn to atoms and to elements; study the earth as a planet or as a structure; look to oceans and continents; trace the development of their living inhabitants; or, finally, read the history of man in structure and powers—one law appears, and one event. We may phrase it as we will, and its expression will vary according to the precise nature of the revelation that is given and according to the temper of him through whom the revelation comes; but beneath all variation there appears, as fundamental to the movement of the entire Kingdom of God, the law which our Lord found in the mustard seed—"it groweth up."

The universe in every part from least to greatest is moving by an inner life; it has growth; it is growing. It has powers and potencies which come into action according to opportunity. They find constant expression in a development after their own kind, according to their own capacity, to ends ordained in them and decreed in their own construction. This is the revelation of the law of the Kingdom of God, operative in all parts of that kingdom, a law whose disclosure has come gradually during the past four centuries, as men have discovered nature, and whose full scope and significance are beginning to be revealed to our own day.

117

Science, Doctor Birge affirmed, is another form of a divine revelation:

Science is teaching men to look for a progressive revelation, to expect from nature new truth, which will call for change and reorganization of former truth. This attitude is nothing new in theory, but it is very far from old in practise, even for individuals. And as present on a large scale, as held by many thousands of thinking men, it now reveals a new and surprising temper and leads to surprising results. Men's eyes are turning to the coming day—to a developing world—as never before. Science inevitably looks to the present and future, to a world unfolding before our eyes—the mustard seed growing up out of the ground. It is sure that the world is "fresh every morning," and that the assurance of the newness requires only eyes to see. It is equally certain that its newness is the natural product of its oldness, that it results from growth, from the new expression of internal powers.

At the close of each creative period God pronounced his work "good." At the end He called it "very good." He has never called it perfect. We talk of the "total depravity of inanimate things," and not without some reason. The Bible tells us that creation has been made subject to vanity, not because it has a wicked will of its own, which thwarts God's will, but by the deliberate will of God, and that the redemption of creation from this subjection to vanity is a part of the hope of the universe. We are living still in the dawn of the creation Sabbath. God seems to be resting from his labors, but really the Father worketh hitherto, and our work is a part of his, and the dew is still on the leaves. This is St. Paul's explanation of much that seems to us awry in the universe. It is awry, he says, but it is not completed. It was made subject to vanity, instability, liability to decay and wrong usage. Nor is it entirely of its own perverseness nor yet of the will of man that it is so; it is in process of completion. It has been so made by a conscious act of God, causing it intentional subjugation to powers from which it is yet to be redeemed. God's plan is to be judged, not alone by the uncompleted work which is now seen, but more by the final redemption of all that He has made. This redemption begins with mankind, and through the revelation of our divine sonship is to be wrought the redemption of creation from the bondage of corruption into the liberty of our own glory as the children of God.

That is, the Bible does not affirm that God started a machine which He has permitted to get beyond his control, and that He is now desperately pursuing it in the almost hopeless effort to regain it. The Bible says that God is on the throne, and ever has been. This is a tremendous assumption, but it is scientific. Paul says the creation, that is, the world, as we know it, is unfinished; it is the germ of the world that is to be. It is coming to the birth. The past is pre-natal. These "vanities" and sins and sorrows are the birth-throes of God's ultimate purpose. There is to be a delivering of the creation, a cosmic redemption.

If we are sure of this, it is no small gain. The method of God is discernible in part, and very perplexing in the parts we do not understand, but there is a soul in the universe, working out a logical result.

Great minds have sometimes endeavored to reproduce the sensation which an intelligent being might have experienced if present at creation. He would have been filled with wonder and reverence at the unfolding of the divine plan—so they assume. But it is more probable that such a mind

120

would have been completely bewildered at the apparent contradictions, the long delays when nothing seemed to be accomplished, and the unnumbered centuries in which the work of creation seemed to have been abandoned by God to the play of wild and conflicting forces. At infinite cost earth crust was formed to be submerged in the seething caldron of eruption and upheaval. Beds of rock which took centuries to form disappeared from sight in a single subsidence. Spots that seemed preparing for an Eden were engulfed in a deluge when the fountains of the great deep were broken up. Forests grew for ages to be buried beneath sand which hardened into rock, and the loss seemed irreparable and inexplicable. We could not have understood it had we seen it in progress. Hence, I say, there has been vast gain that the progress of creation, still incomplete, may now be discerned; that an end, a purpose, or a series of purposes, may now be discovered by an intelligent mind.

Professor N. S. Shaler, in *The Interpretation of Nature,* declared that there has been a perceptible progress among scientists in the recognition of purpose in creation. "In the study of the succession exhibited by plants and animals, it has been perceived that the march of events from the primitive simplicity toward greater and greater complication, culminating in man, requires us to assume the existence of something like permanent guiding influences in the world of matter. . . . In other words, it seems to me that the naturalist is most likely to approach the position of the philosophical theologian by paths which at first seemed to lie far apart from his domain" (pp. 46, 47).

If this be true, and the naturalist and theologian, one working from the standpoint of observed phenomena, and the other from axiomatic or revealed truth, and one by induction and the other by deduction, meet at length like the workmen from the two ends of the Hoosac tunnel, each complementing the work of the other, and each affirming the discovery of what Professor Shaler calls "something like permanent guiding influences" in creation, immense gain has been made that man has been able to discover these purposes; and a new teleological argument of great cogency is added to those formerly in our possession.

A truth is more than doubly valuable when thus doubly discovered. It is valuable for what it is in itself, and for the confidence in both processes which may result in other discoveries. When Leverrier and Adams, in 1846, separately computed the position and orbit of a yet undiscovered planet, and Galle, in Berlin, and Challis, in England, following these calculations, found the planet Neptune through the telescope, the discovery was worth more to science than many separate discoveries, either by mathematical calculation or fortuitous telescopic observation. So when the student of the Bible and the student of natural history come by independent lines of research to substantial agreement upon a truth, the value of that discovery is more than doubled. It shows us that the lines of study which seem to us divergent really focus somewhere, and this gives us reason to believe that our study, fruitful in this instance, will be increasingly so in other discoveries.

If there is one objection offered more frequently than another to faith in a life after death, it is that such a life must be, in all its essential qualities, so far beyond anything we now know, as to be a matter of the imagination only. This seems to ignore the fact that imagination is most commonly thought of as belonging to the sphere of art.

In our exercise of the imagination in the sphere of religion, we are not going beyond what becomes necessary in the sphere of science. Great scientists have recognized this, foremost among them Professor Tyndall, who in the beginning of his second lecture on Light, says what he expresses more fully in his *Fragments of Science*. He says of the true scientist that from the very outset he is dependent on his imagination:

"He can not consider, much less answer, the question, 'What Is Light?' without transporting himself to a world which underlies the sensible one, and out of which in accordance with rigid law, all optical phenomena spring. To realize this sub-sensible world, if I may use the term, the mind must possess a certain pictorial power. It has to visualize the invisible. . . . This conception of physical theory implies, as you perceive, the exercise of the imagination. Do not be afraid of this word. . . . I do not mean a riotous power which deals capriciously with facts, but a well-disciplined power whose sole function it is to form conceptions which the intellect imperatively demands." "He must visualize the invisible." So said Professor Tyndall of the scientist. "He endured as seeing Him who is invisible." So says the Bible of the man of faith. The two sound very much alike; they are alike.

All we are claiming for the super-sensible world is what Professor Tyndall claims for the sub-sensible world. And really these two, and the world of sense, are one world, three in one; and no one of the three is apprehended wholly without the imagination.

All great scientists, therefore, are men of imagination, and hence of faith. I do not wonder that Professor Tyndall thought necessary to warn men of the scientific mind not to be afraid of the word, for some of them do not know how much they owe to their own imagination, and to their faith. I could undertake to add some verses to the eleventh chapter of Hebrews and to place upon the list of the faithful a long roll of names of men of science, whose imagination was that of faith.

By faith Columbus, when he was called of God

to discover a new continent, went out not knowing whither he went. By faith he sailed strange waters, with Cabot, Magellan, Vespucius and Balboa, the heirs with him of the same promise; and they beheld, rising from the waters, new heavens and a new earth, fresh from the hand of God, and bestowed upon men through faith.

By faith Copernicus lifted the earth from its solid base and set it to moving in rhythmic order round the sun; by faith he beheld all the suns and suns of suns with planets in bright array, circling round the throne of God; and this he discovered by faith.

By faith Galileo, when he had been forced to recant, still testified that the earth moves ever at the decree of God; by faith he endured persecution till the mind of his fellow men found its orbit in the same true faith.

By faith La Place understood how the worlds are made from star-dust, and framed by the word of God, so that the things that are seen in the making take their place in the established order of an infinite God of goodness and might.

By faith Newton beheld in the fall of the apple

126

the demonstration of an all-pervading force, operating by the unchanging will of God, so that the worlds are held in place and that not by the things that do appear.

By faith Paracelsus, when he was a-dying, bequeathed to those who followed him an imperfect science, much mixed with error, but left the inspiration of his name to others through whom the indivisible elements of earth and the laws that combine them were made known.

These all died in faith, not receiving the promises, but were persuaded of them and embraced them and moved toward them and bequeathed to others the heritage of their faith.

By faith men suffered persecution, ridicule and poverty, and walked from office to office wearily and in threadbare garb, trying to enlist the sympathy and faith of their fellow men in things the world thought visionary, choosing rather to suffer affliction as the children of faith than to sell their vision for bread.

And as for Huxley and Darwin and Tyndall and Spencer, these, too, were men of faith, and their faith gave substance to the things they hoped for, and led them from experiment to hypothesis, anh from hypothesis to theory, and from theory to discovery, and from faith to sight; these also were the children of faith.

And what shall I more say? For the time would fail me to tell of Stevenson and Fulton, of Morse also and Edison, and Roentgen and Lister, and Cyrus Field and Bell, of Marconi and Wilbur Wright, who through faith made iron float, yoked chariots to the invisible power of steam, caused the human voice to be heard across thousands of miles, brought the mind of man into touch with his fellow man beyond the sea, filled the air with voices inaudible to the ear alone and intelligible only to faith, and lifted the bodies and minds of men on wings of wonder and set them to sailing amid the clouds.

Through faith they built railroads, irrigated deserts, and crossed the trackless ice to the poles, led by faith in the compass and the friendly stars. By faith they subdued climates, overcame hardships, out of weakness were made strong, added to the span of human life, wrought wonders incredible, and filled the world with the news of their achievements that ceased to be wonderful through their incredible certitude.

Now they who do such things see visions of them before they come to pass, and thus are men of faith. And these all, and they who labored with them and before them, lived in faith, and those who died, died in faith, that all who follow may add their knowledge to that which is gone before, and the world by the gift of all men of faith at last shall be made perfect.

Is there a life beyond the grave? The man of sense and of sense alone, sees dust return to dust, and answers, "Death ends all." But life itself makes a tremendous demand on the imagination. Our present life is strange and wonderful past all belief. It requires imagination to account for the present union of matter and spirit in these bodies of ours, for who understands it? And why should it be thought a thing incredible that God should raise the dead?

And when we come to believe in heaven, we still have every appeal to the imagination in making our belief a motive in righteousness. So the Bible tells us in material figures a few things that furnish material for the imagination. The gates of pearl, the streets of gold, the ever-blooming flowers and the trees bearing fruit all the year, the nightless day and the unending song—these are the rare materials for the sanctified imagination, to help us to make real to the soul the things that "eye hath not seen, nor ear heard, neither have entered into the heart of man."

We walk by sight, but not wholly, for we walk by faith. And our appeal for clean streets, for righteous politics, for the uplifting of mankind and for the heaven that God hath prepared for them that love Him, as an appeal to that sanctified imagination which fruits in faith.

So let us rejoice in the glory of the human mind, its power to know, its ability to love and rejoice and its creative strength of will. And with it all, let us cultivate that power of seeing the invisible, of forming and cherishing ideals, and of framing an impelling faith, through the enlightening influence of that great gift of God, which gives substance to things hoped for and affords evidence of things not seen. So shall we add our names to those who endure "as seeing Him who is invisible," and share in the triumph of faith.

And so I am ready to meet the practical man

who asks if religion is not largely concerned with the imagination and admit to him that it is. But I also remind him that all his hope for the betterment of human life, and all his inspiration for the life that is to come, necessitate an appeal to the imagination. And I will go further and say that nowhere is that appeal more sane or practical than within the sphere of religion. Whether it be to make real my brother's hunger to the practical end that he may share my loaf, or whether it be that the soul shall be elevated out of the weary round of the commonplace and find fellowship with the hosts immortal, the appeal is to the imagination. The glorious company of the apostles, the goodly fellowship of the prophets, the noble army of martyrs, these are the inspiring companions of the man with the sanctified imagination. On his ears fall the sweet melodies of the choir invisible, and his solitary race in the lonely arena is cheered by the applause of the cloud of witnesses. And he endures "as seeing Him who is invisible."

Scientists are still discussing the conservation of energy. They are not sure whether there is or is not such a thing as waste in the physical universe.

131

We can afford to wait for their investigation with hearty interest in its result. Meantime, we are assured that much that seems waste is not really so. If fire consumes the wood, the whole mass of the original log can be accounted for in the weight of ashes and smoke and vapor; there is precisely as much matter in the world as there was before. Energy, also, is persistent in many, if not all cases, where it appeared to have been dissipated. If we were to add together that which the lightning flash displays in heat and light and rending power, we should be able to assert that all of it was still conserved in the sum total of creation's forces.

God holds matter cheap. Worlds are to Him as small dust in the balance, and He taketh up the isles as a very little thing. Force is not the most precious thing in God's possession; his is the kingdom and the power; He can utilize the atomic energy we vaguely grope after and speculate about. But character is God's most precious product, and most like Himself. Will God cherish with miserly care his least valuable possessions and cast away what has cost Him Gethsemanes of struggle, Calvaries of divine suffering?

Human reason cries out against this conception of a God parsimonious of his cheapest and wasteful of his best.

"What is most excellent, that, as God is God, is permanent."

The body of man reaches its limit in height and weight. This is a wise and necessary limitation; but no such restriction applies to man's power to learn or to grow in goodness.

One of the most easily understood reasons for immortality is the undying appetite of the soul for knowledge and for love. As we approach the limit of life, it never occurs to us that it is time to fold our arms, close our eyes, and bid farewell to nature, poetry, art and friendship. As long as our faculties permit, we take exactly the same interest in life that we would if we were to go on indefinitely.

As we approach its physical limit we cease to harass ourselves or others much about mere questions of creed. A very few central truths satisfy us. Trust in God, love to man, are enough. We cease to argue and to doubt, but we do not cease to learn. The mind is still alert and the spirit is eager for truth and righteousness. Why should that process not go on forever?

Some good people have been concerned lest the doctrine of evolution should furnish an argument against immortality. At what point in the ascent of man, they ask, did the soul enter into immortal relations with mortal life? That is a question which does not belong to the evolution of the race any more than it belongs to the evolution of each individual in the race. Each person begins with a single cell and ascends in his pre-natal development through stages analogous to those of lower forms. We do not know at what point either in the life of the individual or the race the fœtus becomes human. In a sense it was always human, both racially and individually; in another sense it passes over from lower to higher stages of existence. The problem is not to find the line but to discover the significance of the fact.

Reverent believers in evolution, those who see in it God's way of working, have a new joy in its implications. "It means," they say, "that God was always thinking of me." It means that God's interest in the ascent of life goes as far back as the spiral nebulæ, and then as much further into the unfathomable chaos. Still, God was there, and He was thinking of us. He saw the end from the beginning, and held this as the highest stage of evolution, that man, his masterpiece, was to become capable of knowing God, being like God, and living eternally with God.

We need not demand of modern science that it prove to us the fact of immortality, nor cry out against it as godless if it declares that it has made no such discovery and thinks that it can never do so. Personally, I question whether science as such holds this prerogative. But if science can not prove immortality neither can it disprove it, and there are many scientists who have no desire to undertake that task. Meantime, they have given us valued information about this life. For this they have our thanks. And we have their good will, also, while we seek, in the fields where it may properly be found, the proof of life after death.

CHAPTER IX

SCIENCE concerns itself with phenomena, and endeavors to classify and explain the data of experience in orderly fashion and in accord with fixed methods and reliable principles of cause and effect. Philosophy seeks the unification of all knowledge, and a rational synthesis of all the data of science. Philosophy is, by its etymology, the love of wisdom, but it is more than that. It is the attempt to make wisdom out of what, without her aid, might be mere knowledge. It might be expected or at least hoped that the philosophers would be better able than the scientists to give us a confident approach to a hope of life after death. The philosophers have not all agreed, but in the main they have treated the subject with reverence and with profitable results.

There occur to me seven ways in which people may interpret life. The first is: To say that any

136

attempt to discriminate between good and evil is
subjective; that we have no valid reason to believe
that any such distinction exists in the world; that
all things are equally good and equally pure in the
universe at large; that a thing that is not good for
one purpose is good for another, and that probably
nothing is really good or evil at all; that the terms
good and evil are only our attempt to superimpose
our own subjective and variable judgments on a
universe that is inherently non-ethical. That is the
first way; to my mind an utterly inadequate attempt to account for life and the universe.

The second theory holds that there may be good,
and probably is; that there may be evil, and probably is; at least there exist in the universe such currents and counter-currents as seem to us to be good
and evil; forces which we can not account for except by calling them so; but that to distinguish any
moral purpose in the flux of things is utterly impossible for us; that the forces do not simply coun-
teract each other, but they are a confused mass of
counter-currents, which may or may not come to
an ethical result; and that they have no ultimate
destination as far as we can see; so that while there

is a possibility or even a probability of good and evil, those qualities exist, if they do exist, without discoverable ultimate purpose.

The third is a dualistic philosophy. It affirms that there is good and there is evil, equally divided as day and night are equally divided, two permanent and opposing forces. One of the Chinese philosophies represents this doctrine graphically by a reverse curve carefully drawn through a circle, half of it light and half of it dark. You may draw through such a circle a diameter in any direction through the center, always half will be light and half will be dark. Some of the philosophies and some of the religions of the world, even some that call themselves Christian, are based essentially upon that fundamental hostility. There are Christians who so exalt the devil into a kind of negative God as logically to classify themselves in the category of dualists.

The fourth is the philosophy of pure pessimism, which is to say that the evil in the world is so undeniable, so present in even the best of what men call good, that the Creator (if there be one) is to be judged only by the world which He has made, and we can not know Him to be good or imagine Him to be other than malignant. Presumably the Creator is just as good and just as bad as the world which He has made; and being so, He could not have made the world as bad as it is if He had not been fundamentally bad at heart. Whatever good there is, according to this theory, is just enough to save us from suicide, and the Creator desires us to live that we may suffer a little longer. This is the philosophy of Schopenhauer, and of Nietzsche. This philosophy is growing in some sections of polite society. There is something to be said for it. To my mind there is just enough truth in it to emphasize its utter and infernal folly.

The next is a complete antithesis of the one we have been considering. It holds that God is good and only good and eternally good and there can not enter into his life and into his purpose any conception of evil; and therefore the world is good and only good, and nothing in it can be anything else than good, and we are to deny that anything is evil or that evil could be.

The sixth teaches that God is good and God always has been good, and God always will be good, but the world is bad, as bad at present as it can be; and probably getting worse. But if you ask how a good God could make a bad world, the answer is that it was made good and something happened to it; a snake got in, or the devil—into the garden, or into the heart of a man or a woman, one or both. In the beginning God made all good and something occurred to it to change it, and whether it now can be repaired is the problem of Theology. Some think it is getting better and some think it is getting worse, but the idea is of a perfect world in the beginning, the mirror of the mind of a perfect God, but a world which has met with some moral mishap.

I shall not stop to speak of these six. Each has its stout defenders. All of them to my mind are inadequate.

We come now to the last. It calls for the most faith of any, in that it calls for the most perfect vision of them all. It says that God is good, fundamentally and eternally good, and that He has made a world, the bed rock of which is his own everlasting goodness; that the undeniable evil that is in it is somehow the expression of his goodness; that the world has never got away from Him; that God is

still in the saddle; that God is still on the throne;
God is still King of the world; that even the forces
of evil and unrestraint are under his control,
working out a more glorious form of his eternal
goodness than the world has yet seen. That calls
for no cheap and easy optimism. Over against the
easier, cheaper forms which sing and trip along—

> God's in his heaven
> All's right in the world;

this says, "God is working in his world, and all's
right with his heaven." God made a good world,
but a world that lacked the perfection of moral
character, because character is the one good thing
which God can not furnish ready made. The world
never has been perfect, but is working toward perfection.

There is only one religion that is brave enough
to face all the facts of life, the bitter and the unpleasant facts as well as the facts that are agreeable
and readily intelligible. It is no cheap and easy
optimism which we find in the Bible. It is an
optimism which arrives at its basis of assurance
through conflict; that discovers its certainty of

divine love while looking squarely in the face of the contentions and sorrows of the world.

Swift and violent are the reactions of the human mind in times such as these in which we now live, and great is the temptation to react toward some form of social or spiritual hysteria. Even desirable changes are liable to occur in undesirable ways, and truths neglected to spring up, bound hand and foot with the grave clothes of error. We are in a new era, not only in politics but in religion. It emerged from the chaos of war, and it is still without form and void, and darkness is upon the face of the deep. May the Spirit of God brood upon the waters, and bring to the world order, light and life.

It is not strange that before the War, faith in immortality burned low in the socket. Our studies in science and religion had been almost wholly in other directions, and our philosophy had sought to discover whether it could not somehow modify the declaration of Novalis, that "Philosophy can bake us no bread; but she can procure for us God, freedom and immortality." The baking of bread had become a highly important vocation, and the quest

142

for immortality a neglected pursuit. Philosophy had largely given place to psychology, and psychology was a cheap word in the mouth of the faker. Science had become nothing if not "comparative" and the religious disciplines nothing if not "social." It is said that Agassiz introduced the new order of thinking into modern science in a single sentence in criticism of a new book which his associates at a scientific dinner were commending—"The fatal error of the book is that while it is descriptive it is not comparative." Descriptive works in natural science were thenceforth counted of value only as material for investigation. Comparative anatomy, comparative zoology, comparative psychology became the new order, and the word "comparative" ruled in all sciences dealing with life in any of its forms. The human hand, the human eye, the human brain ceased to be studied as they had been studied in the days of Paley, as proofs of intelligent design on the part of an all-wise and all-good Creator, and assumed their places in the catalogue of comparative forms of evolution, having common origins and diversified adaptations to environment. The hand, for instance, was no longer an argument in natural theology, showing the perfection of God's work in man who was made in the image of God, but was an adaptation of a highly developed form of mammalian life, analogous in its essential anatomical parts to other developments of the quadruped type, and comparable, bone for bone, artery for artery, nerve for nerve, muscle for muscle, with the paw of the lion, the wing of the bird and the flipper of the whale, all of them variant forms of the same generic type. Even religion was no longer to be studied as if there were one true and many false religions, but all religions were to be recognized as the gropings of the human mind after God, if haply they might find Him, who was not far from every one of them. Comparative religion became as essential as comparative anatomy.

Moving in the other direction, religion had rushed with ardor into all manner of social experiment. The Gospel was discovered, not primarily as a preparation for death, but as a rule of life, and that life essentially social. A whole group of new sciences and philosophies sprang into being. We had for the first time social psychology, social

144

ethics, and in a sense, a new social gospel. Washington Gladden and Walter Rauschenbush did not live in vain. Rauschenbush was able before he died to see of the travail of his soul and be satisfied with the widespread preaching of the social Gospel for which earlier he had pleaded, to publish a book lamenting that that social Gospel had as yet no adequate theory, and to attempt himself to furnish the outlines of *A Theology for the Social Gospel.*

Inevitably these studies, theological and scientific as well as philosophical, tended to a pragmatic adaptation of religion to the needs of the present life. "One world at a time" was almost enough for it. A man not much beyond middle age could say, as one did say:

"In my childhood, the preaching was seventy-five per cent about hell, twenty per cent about heaven, and five per cent about this present life. Then came a time when it was seventy-five per cent about heaven, twenty per cent about hell, and the same old five per cent about this life. And now it is ninety per cent about this life, ten per cent about heaven, and hell is a back number."

His percentages may be open to dispute, but the

shifting of emphasis had occurred within his personal recollection. In 1916 Professor James H. Leuba of Bryn Mawr, published a book,* in which he set forth results of inquiries, among college students, scientists and men of standing in the literary world, but especially among the students of one college for women. It was found that only a minority of those whom he had interrogated believed in personal immortality. He believed that faith had little practical value in the life of modern educated people. Holding, as he did, that the real ground for the continuance of this belief in a personal God, was not the validity of the positive proofs, but the practical utility of the beliefs themselves, he challenged the practical utility of the belief, and declared that the answer commonly given to the question of such utility was wholly unconvincing.

Such were the straws that showed some currents of the wind when America entered the World War.

Of the dimming of faith in immortality before the War, and of the way in which the War compelled the world to think of the fact of life and the

*The Belief in God and Immortality: A Psychological, Anthropological and Statistical study. By James H. Leuba. Boston, Sherman, French & Company, 1916.

mystery of death, Dean Inge, of Saint Paul's in London, says:

References to the future life had, before the War, become rare even in the pulpit. The topic was mainly reserved for letters of condolence and was then handled gingerly, as if it would not bear much pressure. Working-class audiences and congregations listened eagerly to the wildest promises of an earthly Utopia the day after to-morrow, but cooled down at once when they were reminded that "if in this life only we have hope in Christ, we are of all men most miserable." Accordingly, the clerical demagogue showed more interest in the unemployed than in the unconverted. Christianity, which began as a revolutionary idealism, had sunk into heralding an apocalyptic revolution. Such teachers have no message of hope and comfort for those who have lost their dearest. And they have, in fact, been deserted. Their secularized Christianty was received with half-contemptuous approval by trade unions, but far deeper hopes, fears, and longings have been stirred, which concern all men and women alike, and on the answers to which the whole value of existence is now seen to depend. Christianity can answer them, but not the Churches through the mouths of their accredited representatives. And so, instead of "the blessed hope of everlasting life," the bereaved have been driven to this pathetic and miserable substitute, the barbaric belief in ghosts and demons, which was old before

147

Christianity was young. And what a starveling hope it is that necromancy offers us! An existence as poor and unsubstantial as that of Homer's Hades, which the shade of Achilles would have been glad to exchange for serfdom to the poorest farmer, and with no guarantee of permanence, even if the power of comforting or terrifying surviving relations is supposed to persist for a few years. Such a prospect would add a new terror to death; and none would desire it for himself. It is plainly the dream of an aching heart, which can not bear to be left alone.—*Survival and Immortality* in *Hibbert Journal.*

The philosophers have not been able to set forth the facts of human life without taking account of man's hope of immortality. They have sought to discover in the realm of pure thought and in the conditions of life, the basis which may exist for such a hope, and to a surprising extent they have given utterance to a firm faith in a life beyond the grave. We have no present purpose to attempt the merest outline of their approach to the subject. Volumes which deal with this aspect of their thinking are reasonably abundant. We may, however, refresh our memory with a glance at the method of reasoning of some of the leading thinkers of ancient and of modern times.

We begin with Plato, remembering that in his writings we have also the teaching of Socrates.

Plato believed that the soul had existence before it entered the life of this world. His belief in a future life was joined to a belief that life had passed through a previous existence. Plato held that immortality is not a doctrine for philosophy so much as it is for theology. He does however attempt an explanation. God, he says, is good, and free from all jealousy. He wants the largest possible number of beings to share his perfection. Upon the beings thus created, God confers the eternity which of right belongs to Him alone. This is a very close approach to the Christian doctrine of God, "Who only hath immortality, dwelling in the light which no man can approach unto;" (I Timothy 6:16), but who has freely granted this quality of his own perfection to those whom He has made in his own image.

To be sure, Plato does not always deal with the subject on this high level of assurance. In his *Apology,* his *Phædo,* his *Republic* and his *Phædrus* he approached the question from different angles, and at times seemed to be less convinced by his own reasoning; but this only shows how many angles of approach this philosopher found and his effort to explore each avenue honestly to its own proper ending.

The philosophy of Socrates has been considered in some respects agnostic. That term should not be accepted either in his case or in that of the men who in the beginning applied it to their own position as implying any degree of disinclination to believe. It was to him and to many of them the attitude of the open mind. When Socrates was condemned to death, he faced his judges and calmly accepted his sentence. In a brief and most memorable speech he said to them that, while they had not so intended it, they were doing him a kindness. If death was a dreamless sleep, as some supposed, that would bring him relief from many trials and cares, and crown a life which he was content to look back upon without regret. But he thought it possible that death was not a sleep, but a new life in Hades, in which event he would have opportunity to converse with Rhadamanthus and with the heroes and sages of all past ages. If death were but a sleep, his judges had done him a kindness; if it should prove indeed a new life, then great would be his gain.

Calm in this assurance, he lived the thirty days that, under the unusual conditions of his sentence, he had to live, received his friends, conversed on high themes, refused all proposals made by his friends that would have enabled him to escape, and met death on the high plane of a serene confidence that all was well with him.

Of modern philosophy, the fountain head is Immanuel Kant. He did not regard immortality as proved by pure reason, but he reached assurance by what he called practical reason. He sought, as did Plato and Socrates, the *summum bonum,* or highest good for man. How is man to know that good and attain it? Man has in him conscience, which does not say, "This is desirable," but "This is what you must do, or fail of your duty." The characteristic of conscience is its assumption of authority, its categorical imperative. This conscience possessed by man is nothing more nor less than the indwelling life of God. It is of the nature of Reason, but it is in itself unreasonable, unless there is a God from whom it proceeds, and who will give opportunity for it to realize its fruition. But that opportunity can not be realized in a limited life such as we lead here. The God who has put within us the expression of his own life in the categorical imperative will provide adequate life for its realization. This is Kant's argument in his own words:

The realization of the *summum bonum* in the world is the necessary object of a will determinable by the moral law. But in this will the *perfect accordance* of the mind with the moral law is the supreme condition of the *summum bonum*. This then must be possible, as well as its object, since it is contained in the command to promote the latter. Now, the perfect accordance of the will with the moral law is *holiness,* a perfection of which no rational being of the sensible world is capable at any moment of his existence. Since, nevertheless, it is required as practically necessary, it can only be found in a *progress in infinitum* toward that perfect accordance, and on the principles of pure practical reason it is necessary to assume such a practical progress as the real object of our will.

Now, this endless progress is only possible on the supposition of an *endless* duration of the *existence* and personality of the same rational being (which is called the immortality of the soul). The *summum bonum,* then, practically is only possible on the supposition of the immortality of the soul; consequently this immortality, being inseparably connected with the moral law, is a postulate of pure practical reason (by which I mean a *theoretical* proposition, not demonstrable as such, but which is

152

an inseparable result of an unconditioned *a priori* practical law).*

And again:

In the foregoing analysis the moral law led to a practical problem which is prescribed by pure reason alone, without the aid of any sensible motives, namely, that of the necessary completeness of the first and principal element of the *summum bonum,* viz. Morality; and as this can be perfectly solved only in eternity, to the postulate of *immortality.* The same law must also lead us to affirm the possibility of the second element of the *summum bonum,* viz. Happiness proportioned to that morality, and this on grounds as disinterested as before, and solely from impartial reason; that is, it must lead to the supposition of the existence of a cause adequate to this effect; in other words, it must postulate the *Existence of God,* as the necessary condition of the possibility of the *summum bonum* (an object of the will which is necessarily connected with the moral legislation of pure reason). . . . The postulate of the possibility of the *highest derived good* (the best world) is likewise the postulate of the reality of a *highest original good,* that is to say, of the existence of God. Now it was seen to be a duty for us to promote the *summum bonum;* consequently it is not merely allowable, but it is a necessity connected with duty as a requisite, that we should presuppose the possibility of this *summum bonum;* and as this is possible only on con-

*Crit. of Pract. Reason, bk. ii., ch. ii., § iv., trans. Abbott.

dition of the existence of God, it inseparably connects the supposition of this with duty; that is, it is morally necessary to assume the existence of God.*

True philosophy is not content with an immortality which is survival and nothing more. It demands an immortality that gives full opportunity for the expression of the exuberance of human life. Of that life as here manifest, William James wrote:

Man's chief difference from the brutes lies in the exuberant excess of his subjective propensities—his preeminence over them simply and solely in the number and in the fantastic and unnecessary character of his wants, physical, moral, esthetic, and intellectual. Had his whole life not been a quest for the superfluous he would never have established himself as inexpugnably as he has done in the necessary. And from the consciousness of this he should draw the lesson that his wants are to be trusted; that even when their gratification seems farthest off, the uneasiness they occasion is still the best guide of his life and will lead him to issues entirely beyond his present powers of reckoning. Prune down his extravagance, sober him, and you undo him. The appetite for immediate consistency at any cost, or what the logicians call the "law of parsimony"—which is nothing but the passion for conceiving the universe in the most labor-saving

*Ibid., § v.

way—will, if made the exclusive law of the mind, end by blighting the development of the intellect itself quite as much as that of the feeling or the will. The scientific conception of the world as an army of molecules gratifies this appetite after its fashion most exquisitely. But if the religion of exclusive scientificism should ever succeed in suffocating all other appetites out of a nation's mind, and imbuing a whole race with the persuasion that simplicity and consistency demand a tabula rasa to be made of every notion that does not form part of the soi-disant scientific synthesis, that nation, that race, will just as surely go to ruin and fall a prey to their more richly constituted neighbors, as the beasts of the field, as a whole, have fallen a prey to man.

In the face of life's stupendous mysteries, we can afford to be very modest in our affirmations, and charitable toward those who do not share our confidence. Too often men have been condemned as atheists who were at the worst agnostics. They have suffered the opprobrium of harsh names when they should at least have been credited with honesty in refusing to affirm doctrines which, sometimes reluctantly, they found themselves impelled to doubt. Faith in immortality is a precious possession to him who is able to afford it; but even more precious than faith is charity. No man having faith in immortality gains by that faith the right to be censorious toward those who doubt.

Even the doubters have their faith. None of us is consistent, least of all can those be consistent who deal in negations. Sooner or later hope rises above denial, and hope is akin to faith.

I am not sure that we have any right to divide men into groups of believers and infidels. Some of those who believe have never had faith enough to nourish a doubt; and some of those who doubt might prompt the Lord to say, "I have not found so great faith, no not in Israel."

Colonel Robert G. Ingersoll was an orator, not a scholar; a poet rather than a philosopher. Yet he had what may be called his philosophy of the future life. Called to speak at the grave of his brother, and again at the grave of a friend, and still again at the grave of a little child, he uttered what was his personal creed, the right to hope for the best:

"We, too, have our religion, and it is this: Help for the living—Hope for the dead."

He did not pretend to know:

"Every cradle asks us 'Whence?' and every coffin, 'Whither?' The poor barbarian, weeping

156

above his dead, can answer these questions just as well as the robed priest of the most authentic creed."

"In the presence of death, how beliefs and dogmas wither and decay! How loving words and deeds burst into blossom! All wish for happiness beyond this life. All hope to meet again the loved and lost. In every heart there grows this sacred flower. Immortality is a word that Hope through all the ages has been whispering to Love. Let us believe that over the cradle Nature bends and smiles, and lovingly above the dead in benediction holds her outstretched hands."

"Life is a narrow vale between the cold and barren peaks of two eternities. We strive in vain to look beyond the heights. We cry aloud, and the only answer is the echo of our wailing cry. From the voiceless lips of our unreplying dead there comes no word; but in the night of death Hope sees a star, and listening Love can hear the rustle of a wing."

These are sentences quoted from his addresses at the grave. Shall we say that under stress of emotion he contradicted the negations of his own creed? It would not be fair thus to accuse him. Rather it would be more true to say that he himself did not regard these hopes based on love as a

157

denial of his every day creed. He did not know, but he hoped.

Of a friend who died, sharing his doubt and faith, he said:

"He lived for this world: if there be another, he will live for that."

He maintained that we do not know whether death is a wall or a door; the beginning or the end of a day; the folding forever of wings, or the spreading of pinions to soar; the rise or set of a sun; the quiet end of life or the beginning of an endless life that brings the rapture of love. Of this he was sure, that immortality must be more than a continuity of life: it must bring recognition and love:

"I had rather live and love where death is king than have eternal life where love is not. Another life is naught unless we know and love again the ones who love us here."

But he would not live on negations:

"Whatever flower of hope springs in my heart I will cherish; I will give it breath of sighs and rain of tears."

158

When he was told that he had been accused of attempting to destroy men's faith in immortality, he denied it. Immortality, he said, was a hope that no man could destroy, and he had no desire to destroy it: it was a hope that sprang from Love and would persist so long as Love reached out its hand and held to the cold hand of Death. But are we to meet and know our loved ones?

"Reason says, 'Perhaps,' and Hope whispers, 'Yes.'"

There is a sense in which we are all philosophers by compulsion. We can not restrain ourselves from asking the reasons for things and seeking to unify our little broken knowledge.

If a man were to spend his life beside the Niagara River and had little knowledge of geography or natural science, but was possessed of reasonable intelligence, he would find himself continually meditating about the river whose waters were flowing past him, by day and by night, and would ask himself, "Where does this water come from, and where does it go to?" He would observe that the stream flowed ever in one direction; that it never reversed its current; that it flowed gently at the upper end of the short stream, but gathered momentum, and moved more and more swiftly, until at last with terrific speed it plunged over the edge of the chasm, to be lost below in the whirlpool and swallowed up in a vast mystery.

He would sometimes ask himself, "Is there any power on earth that can lift those waters up again to their former level above the Falls?" He would be very likely to answer that there can be no such power. He could hardly be expected to think otherwise. He could see nothing, understand nothing, to justify any other opinion. The water flowed down from an unknown source, running faster and faster, until at last it disappeared over the Falls, and that was virtually the end of it. It flowed on to unseen mysteries, but it came back never. He might even come to see a certain fascination in it, think it a desirable arrangement, and lose all wish to have it otherwise.

But even as he looked, the water would be rising. He could not see it or understand it, but the very mist into which the falling water was dashed, would be the beginning of its elevation. And if he could but know it, the silent power of the sun playing upon it was able to lift it up, not simply to its

160

former level at the brink of the chasm, but higher than the river, higher than the lake above the river, up and up, into the very sky, where rainbows would play through it, and the sunlight find joy in its companionship. And in time, it would be sent on fresh ministries, unending opportunities of service.

We live on the banks of such a stream. Its waters flow ever in one direction. They go faster and faster as the years multiply, and they take a plunge which carries them from our sight. That river is the stream of human life. We may not sit upon its banks, for we flow with it and are a part of it; but we are able to see the direction of its current and to witness the plunge before we ourselves take it. We are compelled to ask ourselves again and again, What is the source of life, and what is its destiny?

It is not strange that our first answer should be that death ends all. It is not to be wondered that we see no great distance down the gorge or beyond the whirlpool. The wonder is that we see as much as we do, or that we possess as much faith as we know ourselves to have.

But the power of God that lifts the water out of the cataract, out of the whirlpool, out of the very ocean, and sends it, purified and illumined, on other ministries, is capable of lifting human life out of the grave, and giving to it new opportunity, new service, new light and life.

A rational hope of immortality involves the survival of personality and the continued existence of personal identity. There will be recognition of loved ones, and a permanence of social relationships. We shall not be impersonal units in a celestial mob, and our friends will not be lost to us in the unnumbered and unidentified multitude.

Let us carry this thought further in the relation of this present life to the life to come. I shall not lead you into any of those fantastic, and to my mind, unworthy imaginings which of late have become common; neither shall we go wholly into the realm of speculative theology. I am proposing to outline my own approach to a study of this subject. I do not claim that this line of thought is original with me; it is in essential accord with that set forth by the eminent physician of three hundred years ago, Sir Thomas Browne. It is also that which was developed by Gustav Theodor Fechner who was not a theologian but whose province was

162

physics and psychology. His work in cosmogony and in the study of electrical energy and the validity of the atomic theory has made him an authority in those departments of research. He was also a very direct and practical philosopher.

Following a line of thought parallel with Fechner, and in places essentially the same as his, I give my own confession of faith in terms of a philosophic interpretation of life and hope.

We live, in this life of which our conscious earth-experience is a part, not once, but certainly twice, and I rather think three times. We are living now, and we know it. We have lived previously, and we just as certainly know that, and we have what I believe are valid hopes for a life to come.

Compare for a few moments the life we now have with that which we know we formerly possessed. We need not go into those fine and suggestive uncertainties so beautifully set forth by Wordsworth:

> Our birth is but a sleep and a forgetting:
> The soul that rises with us, our life's star,
>   Hath elsewhere had its setting,
>   And cometh from afar.
> Not in entire forgetfulness,
> And not in utter nakedness,

163

But trailing clouds of glory, do we come
From God, who is our home!
Heaven lies about us in our infancy.

Such thoughts move us profoundly by their beauty and suggestiveness. We seek to fathom our own souls, and look deep into the eyes of children to discover if they may be true.

But we are to keep close to the simple facts as we know them, and we say, The life that we are now living is part and parcel of a life which had a previous existence, and we know it. We are to think for a few minutes about that previous life of ours, that it may provide us whatever suggestions it affords of another life.

Every one who now is here lived on earth before. We lived lives that are plainly continued in this life, lives for which that form of life was a preparation. For the space of some ten lunar months each one of us lived in that previous state. Now, for varying periods—in some instances as many as three score years and ten—we have lived somewhat as we now are living.

In the first stage, man lives alone in the darkness; in the second, he lives in association with companions and friends; in the third stage he is to live in a higher social sphere, in which we shall know perfectly, even as we are known, and discern ultimate verities.

Our previous life was a continuous sleep; our present life alternates between sleeping and waking; the coming stage of our life will be of everlasting consciousness.

The function of the first stage was to prepare a body and brain suited to the second stage; and the function of the second is to develop a character fitted for the third.

Now, in the first stage, we had eyes that never opened, and which, if they had opened, could have seen nothing; but those eyes that were formed in darkness were formed for the light. In the first stage we had ears that never heard a sound, but though formed in the silence, they were made for hearing. All the light of the seven colors of the spectrum, all the sounds and chords of the octave, were created for eyes and ears that were made in darkness and silence.

It seems to me quite impossible that the little unborn child should have any premonition of the pur-

165

pose for which it is living and is to live; but if we could imagine it to be possible that through the telepathy of love the little life might ask of its mother, "Are these parts of me which have no present use made for any use hereafter?" the mother would whisper, "Yes, my dear little one, your eyes are forming to behold beautiful things, and your ears are so created as to enjoy rich harmonies, and your tiny hands and feet are for a world where you can use and enjoy them and do useful things with them; and if I can not tell you everything that you would like to know, believe the best that you possibly can believe; it is all true, and more."

There are two transitions from one to another of these three stages of our life. Both are through darkness and pain. The first of them we call birth; the other we call death. As we could not adequately interpret the first before our birth, so neither can we fully understand that the darkness and pain of death are the way to light and joy, but it is true.

To what extent is it true that life is continuous through all these stages? The body which we now have is the same body that we had before we were born, taller and larger and modified by growth and

contact with the world, but the same. Are we to
believe in the resurrection of the body?

The ancient creeds say, "I believe in the resurrection of the body." Personally, I prefer not to
be asked to express my own faith in those precise
words. I should prefer that whatever creeds I am
asked to recite should be formulated as nearly as
may be in terms of the thought of my own generation. But this may not always be. If we are to
recite our faith in unison with other Christians we
must be allowed all reasonable elasticity in the use
of words. The makers of the old creeds knew no
possibility of personal survival apart from the
body. When they said, "I believe in the resurrection of the body," they meant, "I believe in the survival of personal identity." If I find myself in a
congregation which is using such a creed I do not
forbear to recite the words with them, but I believe,
and I think they also believe, in general, what the
makers of the creed meant, the survival of personality.

As to the survival of the physical body, let us
employ an illustration which seems to me suggestive.

It is not quite true that the body which we now

have is identical in its parts with what constituted
the body of the unborn child. In the embryonic
period it was only a part of his body, and in the
early stages of life, a minor part. The other part
enveloped it, and gave it life. The two developed
together, and the two were born together. But
they were soon separated, and the part that had
been so useful was discarded immediately as being
no longer of use. No one cared very much what
became of that discarded envelope that had belonged to the body. It was buried soon and without grief. No one ever desired that it should
return to cumber a body which it had once sup-
ported but which had become capable of independent existence.

Now, I suppose that if the unborn child could be
told that as soon as it was born its body would be
cut in two and one part discarded and buried, never
to rise again, the little infant mind would be
stricken with terror. How could it possibly live
without that part of its being which it had always
possessed, and which had furnished it its very life
blood and sustenance? The little mind might even
try to formulate a foolish creed affirming its belief

168

in the permanent survival of all that it regarded as its body, all that it had found essential to its life and well-being. I suppose we are not much more capable of making wise creeds that dogmatize about the relations of this physical body to the spiritual life. It is enough for us to know that personality will survive, and will evolve for its spiritual uses an organism suited to its continued life.

I think of this present wonderful body of ours as a kind of placenta for the spiritual organism that shall relate itself to our spiritual life and express our spiritual nature in the world to come. I do not despise these beautiful bodies of ours, but I like to think that our spiritual life is capable of developing for its expression an organism as well adapted to its future existence as this one is to our present existence. This present body is but the placenta of the spiritual organism that is to be.

The immortality which the best of our philosophers teach is an immortality which recognizes the unlimited capacity of the human soul for growth; its capacity for joy, for love, for goodness. It gives us not life, merely, but life more abundant.

We can not claim that philosophy has given to us

a demonstration of immortality; that would be too much to ask; but it does give to us the assurance that faith in immortality is reasonable, as judged by the tests of sound and sane thinking. It enables us to go back over the history of human thought and say with Addison:

It must be so—Plato, thou reasonest well—
Else whence this pleasing hope, this fond desire,
This longing after immortality?
　Or whence this secret dread, and inward horror,
Of falling into naught? Why shrinks the soul
Back on herself and startles at destruction?
'Tis the divinity that stirs within us;
'Tis Heaven itself that points out an hereafter
And intimates Eternity to man.

CHAPTER X

IMMORTALITY IN THE OLD TESTAMENT

CONSIDERING that some of the fathers of the Jewish nation lived in Egypt, and that Egypt was never far away from their place of sojourn, it is nothing less than remarkable that the Old Testament contains so little about immortality. The Tel el-Amarna letters show us that in the centuries almost immediately preceding the occupancy of Palestine by the people of Israel, that land was ruled by Egypt: it is strange that Egyptian religion left there no notable mark of its own faith in the survival of the soul.

Let us see if we can find immortality in the Old Testament.

The doctrine of personal immortality is not taught in the Law of Moses.

The doctrine of life after death is not taught in the prophets. When Isaiah, greatest of all the

171

prophets, went to see Hezekiah, who was sick, he
had no message of everlasting life with which to
comfort him. And when Hezekiah later recorded
the prayer he made to God, and which God heard
for his recovery, it was a prayer which contained a
distinct denial of immortality.

For the grave can not praise thee, death can not
    celebrate thee:
They that go down into the pit can not hope for thy
    truth.
The living, the living; he shall praise thee, as I do
    this day:
The father to the children shall make known thy
    truth.—Isaiah 38:18-20.

For a long time the doctrine held was that a man
was to survive in his posterity, or in his nation. It
was believed that the righteous were to prosper in
health and wealth, and the wicked to be punished
with adversity during their life.

But there are two great skeptical books which
deny this doctrine and through their doubt come to
a vague affirmation of immortality. One of these
is Ecclesiastes, which first denies that there is any
difference between the fate of the good and the
bad, between man and the brute; but at length

172

comes out of this pessimism into a conviction that a man should remember his Creator in youth, before such pessimism comes to him, and that when the dust returns to the earth as it was, the spirit shall return to God who gave it.

There is dim light in the other great book of doubt and faith, the book of Job. Job's friends defend the traditional theology, which asserts that God rewards the just and punishes the evil in this life, and Job knows that is not true in his case. So he affirms that if this is God's method, God is making a mistake in this particular instance, and he appeals to the God back of his god, from god to God, from the god of phenomena to the God of justice and truth; from the god "who hath taken away my right" to the God who is next of kin to an honest man. At first he has no faith in immortality, nor in the divine justice.

He declares that his friends are wrong when they assert that God prospers good men and brings bad men to naught, for the tents of robbers prosper, and the good man is made a laughing-stock. And neither he nor his friends have any faith in a hereafter save one in which souls shall live in a low

173

subconscious state, the good and the evil and the untimely born together, in unconsciousness of each other, even of those nearest to them, while they suffer little and scarcely realize pain.

Daniel, which is a very late book, and one which the Hebrews never reckoned among the prophets, has this affirmation:

And many of them that sleep in the dust of the earth shall awake, some to everlasting life, and some to shame and everlasting contempt.—Daniel 12:2.

This is perhaps the clearest passage in the Old Testament, and the only one with a distinct message of retribution for evil. But this is very late.

The Psalms seem to deny and then to affirm immortality. They are the work of many authors, covering several centuries in their composition. Psalm VI is the song of a sick man, a pathetic cry of pain, pleading with God for recovery. It says:

For in death there is no remembrance of thee: in the grave who shall give thee thanks?—Psalm 6:5.

Psalm XXX is a song of praise for recovery, probably by the same writer, and expresses the same measure of faith:

I cried to thee, O Lord; and unto the Lord I made supplication. What profit is there in my blood, when I go down to the pit? Shall the dust praise thee? Shall it declare thy truth?—Psalm 30:8-9.

Even as late as the Exile some singers of Israel have no hope of life after death. One of them cries out to God to save his people from the captivity before they all die in Babylon, and go to where God forgets people:

Wilt thou shew wonders to the dead? Shall the dead arise and praise thee? Shall thy loving kindness be declared in the grave? or thy faithfulness in destruction?—Psalm 88:10-11.

But two earlier Psalms have a clearer faith. One of the authors has his lines cast in pleasant places and is sure that God's goodness will continue:

Therefore my heart is glad, and my glory rejoiceth: my flesh also shall rest in hope.
For thou wilt not leave my soul in hell; neither wilt thou suffer thine Holy One to see corruption.
Thou wilt shew me the path of life: in thy presence is fullness of joy; at thy right hand there are pleasures for evermore.—Psalm 16:9-11.

The other singer is in sorrow and oppression, his lot in striking contrast with that of the wicked, who have plenty for themselves and much to leave to their abundant posterity. But this Psalmist says:

From men which are thy hand, O Lord, from men of the world, which have their portion in this life, and whose belly thou fillest with thy hid treasure: they are full of children, and leave the rest of their substance to their babes.

As for me, I will behold thy face in righteousness: I shall be satisfied, when I awake, with thy likeness.—Psalm 17:14-15.

Hegel, in his notable posthumus work on the *Philosophy of Religion,* said:

They (the Jews) did not believe in immortality, for even though it is perhaps possible to point to certain traces of belief in it, still those passages in which they occur are always of a very general character, and had not the slightest influence on the religious and moral points of view from which things were regarded. The immortality of the soul is not yet an admitted truth. . . .*

Professor A. B. Davidson, a noted English Old Testament scholar, said:

If . . . we find explicit teaching on this question of immortality postponed, we may infer that it was not unnatural that it should be so, that there was something in the ways of thinking of the peo-

*Vol. II, p. 213.

ple which, for a time at least, supplied the place of it, or at all events made it not a necessity to a true life with God.*

Reverend C. J. Wright, in a thoughtful article in the *Homiletic Review,* said:

No one should be surprised to find that the Old Testament contains no speculation as to the pre-existence of souls or of metempsychosis. But very many are surprised, when they come to study carefully the teaching of the Old Testament on the subject of the future, to find how vague and indefinite that teaching is, how very slightly emphasized. Here may we say that we are speaking of the eschatology of the individual, and not of the eschatology of the people. The former question is tantamount to that of the doctrine of immortality, the latter to that of the kingdom of God upon earth. The obscurity of our subject as exhibited in the Old Testament is at once acknowledged by all who make it their business to study the question, and the acknowledgment gives rise to many questions. It has been concluded, for example, that the revelation of the truth was kept back by God from his people for certain definite reasons—there may have been danger, for instance, in such a doctrine to the Jews. On this point it has to be remembered that there can be an immoral eschatology; the history of ancient Egyptian religion on this matter is

---

Biblical and Literary Essays, p. 278.

at once significant. But attempts at explanation such as this, while no doubt containing ideas that have kernels of truth within them, seem to conceive of revelation in a more artificial manner than the history of religions warrants.

To the Jew, the idea of personality which we possess was more or less intangible. He had not much regard for individual life; he lived in his family, his tribe, his nation. "Thou shalt love thy clansman as thyself" was the second article in the law for him. The Jew did not think so much of his personal future as of the future of his family.

But he had his own idea of personality. It was not of the soul as distinct from the body: all his expressions of intellectual and emotional activity were assigned by him to some physical organ, the heart, the reins, the bowels. The body was as essential to life, present and prospective, as was any conception which he may have had of the soul. There was no duality between the two in the men who wrote the Old Testament.

We are disposed to relegate rewards and punishments to a future life. Not so the Jew. The book of Proverbs correctly sets forth the Jewish idea that righteousness produces prosperity, and sin brings present and temporal disaster.

The book of Job is written to confute this prevalent idea. It grew out of the conflict between traditional theology and the stern facts of experience.

But if the Jew was not a believer in personal immortality neither did he believe in annihilation. He believed that at death all human lives continued in a place called "Sheol." This word occurs some sixty-five times in the Old Testament. The picture presented by it is so gloomy that the authorized version commonly translated it "hell." But it was not a place of punishment of the evil as contrasted with the reward of the good. A few times where this translation was impossible they gave it the rendering "grave" or "pit." The essential thing to remember about it is that all souls went there without moral distinction. It was a shadowy place, where individual lives continued a kind of existence. It was a place prepared as a "house of meeting for all living." (Job 30:23). It is "a land of darkness and of the shadow of death, without any order, and where the light is as darkness." (Job

179

10:21-22.) It is a place of low consciousness, with little perception of what is happening elsewhere, a place of dull pain and of twilight of the senses. Of the man who is in that place Job said:

His sons come to honor, and he knoweth it not;
And they are brought low, but he perceiveth it not
    of them.
Only for himself his flesh hath pain,
And for himself his soul mourneth.—Job 14:21-22.

Sheol is a place without any moral quality. It was conceived by the Jews as a place where there was bare consciousness and perpetual gloom, but not a place of punishment for sin.

The Preacher says: "The living know that they shall die, but the dead know not anything, neither have they any more a reward. Neither have they any more a portion forever in anything that is done under the sun."—(Eccl. 9:5-6.) Job in one of the most despairing passages in the Old Testament says: "There is hope of a tree if it be cut down, that it will sprout again, and that the tender branch thereof will not cease . . . But man dieth and wasteth away. Yea, man giveth up the ghost and where is he? As the waters fail from the sea, and the river decayeth and drieth up, so man lieth down and riseth not. Till the heavens be no more, they shall not awake, nor be roused out of their sleep." (Job 14:7-12.) What gave Sheol its acutest sting was that there the relations with God were cut off. So the Psalmist cries (6:5), "In death there is no remembrance of thee, In Sheol who shall give thee thanks?" (Psalm 6:5.)

Faith in immortality did not come into the Old Testament till some of its inspired writers passed through experiences, personal and national, which showed them the inadequacy of the doctrine they had been holding. The righteous did not always prosper. Misfortune was not always caused by the sin of the man who suffered it. If God was to deal justly with men, there must be another world in which He could right the wrongs of this. And so, some of them came to believe in a life beyond death.

Jewish thought rose to a conception of the majesty and eternity of God which sometimes swept into its deep current a faith in the eternity of man. Habakkuk cried out:

"Art thou not from everlasting, O Lord my God,

mine Holy One? we shall not die." This would almost seem to identify the believer with God, in his possession of immortality.

There are a few more passages, a very few, and they are of less importance and less clear meaning. Do they afford us faith in immortality? Yes, a dim hope. In them we think we have eternal life. We have a mighty and increasing hope for the Christ. We can find that prophetic hope there without question. In the New Testament we find the Christ himself. And in Him we have, we do not think we have, *we have* eternal life.

CHAPTER XI

IMMORTALITY IN THE NEW TESTAMENT

THE faith which dimly glows in the Old Testament breaks forth in the New Testament into luminous truth. Jesus himself is the light that illumines the sacred Scriptures of the New Covenant.

Jesus recognized that the Old Testament hope of immortality was not very bright. He said to the Jews who were ardent students of the Old Testament, but rejected Him, that it was in Him and not in the letter of the older scriptures that their hope of immortality was to find its assurance. He said, "Search the scriptures; for in them ye think ye have eternal life: and they are they which testify of me. And ye will not come to me, that ye might have life."

We utterly miss the force of these words when we endeavor to strain them into an injunction to

183

read the Bible. The Bible had no readers so dili-
gent as those whom Jesus was addressing. No men
on earth had so little need to be told "search the
scriptures." They did nothing else. And we do
not need this verse as such admonition, for we have
it elsewhere. But we do need the passage in its
true meaning.

Jesus stated as a matter of fact that the men
whom he addressed searched the scriptures. He
neither commanded it nor commended it. He certainly did not reprove it, but He said that in this
particular instance the searching of the scriptures
was not yielding profitable results.

Prophecy, the living voice of aspiration and
faith, was dead. The scribes, who had done so
much to preserve the scriptures, were halting their
inquiry into truth where the prophets left off
speaking. Jesus told the Jews why they searched
the scriptures. It was because in them they thought
they found eternal life. One sect of the Jewish
teachers, the Pharisees, thought they found eternal
life in the Old Testament; another, the Sadducees,
denied it. But Jesus declared that He himself was
the life they sought.

The New Testament doctrine of immortality rests securely on the conviction that this world was created and is governed by a wise and good God. The spirit and character of that God, we discern in Jesus Christ. In Him some men discover a revelation of what God is like, and others find in Him a suggestion of what man may become. I waste no time in discussing the divinity and humanity of Christ. Of this I am sure: I need both aspects of his character. I want to be sure that God is the kind of God whose human coefficient we have in Jesus. Also I want to be sure that the character of Jesus is revealed to me, not for my eternal discomfiture, not to condemn me because I can never hope to be like Him, but for my comfort and encouragement. I believe that we can be like Him. I believe that this is the essential truth of what St. Paul called the Gospel—that the life of God, which was lived humanly by Jesus of Nazareth, can be lived divinely by those who find God in Him.

If that is true, then any good thing may be true. If God is our heavenly Father, and Jesus Christ is the human expression of the character of

185

God and of his attitude toward man, then the only limit of what we may attain is to be found in the limitations which we impose upon ourselves. God has made us in his own image. He has sent our Lord Christ to reveal to us the moral and spiritual implications of that relationship. If God is really our Father, then there is nothing too good to be true.

I do not wonder that the hope of immortality is a hope and not a demonstration. I wonder that so vast and all but incredible a hope should ever have suggested itself or been suggested to us.

But we have such hope, an ineradicable, an indefeasible hope. And if God is good, it is not an unreasonable hope. It is a hope to be examined in the light of our conviction that we live under the rulership of a God whose moral attributes and whose attitude toward humanity we are discovering in Jesus Christ. On the basis of our conviction that we have such a God, our faith in immortality is as reasonable as it is persistent.

There are some utterances of Jesus on this subject which seem to me to be in themselves vast revelations of what it is reasonable for us to hope and believe. Take, for instance, those words which he addressed to his disciples in the Upper Room, when, speaking of life after death, He said: "If it were not so, I would have told you."— John 14:2.

I am inclined to think that we ought to consider these words as among the most precious of all the utterances of Jesus. They are our assurance of the validity of all our most cherished hopes for the life to come; they are the guarantee of our right to believe all that is best and most beautiful concerning our loved ones on the other side.

Jesus had never previously conversed with his disciples on this high theme, yet He assumed that most wonderful things concerning it were or reasonably might be already believed by them, and He declared that these were true. It was as if He said, "Of course such fine things must be true; it could not be otherwise. You should know that without my telling you." It gives us added reason to believe that every beautiful thing we think about Heaven is either true or the suggestion of a truth more beautiful. It confirms us in the faith that all our best endeavors to know about the life to come

187

are founded upon a valid impulse of the human heart. God has not given us these hopes in order to deceive us. The best that we can think is either true or a suggestion of a truth which is better than our thought. We question, we wonder, we doubt, and we express a hesitating faith. "Lord, is this true?" "Certainly it is true," says the spirit of this declaration. "If it were not so, I would have told you." Jesus would not have permitted us to be deceived about anything so important as this. The broken heart of humanity cries out for immortality, and wants to know whether this is a thing too great for us to ask of God. Jesus says that we are permitted to believe in immortality, and that that belief is a true belief. "If it were not so, I would have told you."

The principle underlying this affirmation goes much further than we shall attempt to discover in this chapter. It reminds us that the words of Jesus are to be interpreted more liberally than some people suppose. There are many things desirable for us to know which the Bible does not in so many words tell us. There were many problems confronting the early Church on which Jesus left no specific direction. He did not, so far as we know, leave with his disciples any explicit directions as to the form of organization of the Church, nor any command as to the change of the Sabbath from the seventh to the first day of the week, nor did He indicate in definite terms what reforms Christian men ought in any particular age to champion. Jesus was not a law-giver but a life-giver. He came that men might have life, and live it out in terms of all the best possible in the successive ages in which they were to live. We may search the Bible in vain for a verse that tells us that this is the day or year in which Christian men ought to engage in a particular enterprise or support a particular reform, but the Spirit of Jesus is with us to say, "Of course you should do this good thing; if it were not so, I would have told you." I do not like to say that Jesus has left us to work these problems out for ourselves, because that is not what I believe. He has not left us. His spirit is still with us to guide us in all matters which are vital to the progress of the work of Christ in the world.

I mention these matters only as a passing suggestion, and I shall not return to them. They illustrate in what and how many interesting directions a verse like this might carry us. But I think it profoundly significant in its assurance of the fact and the character of immortality.

When I think of immortality, I remember the old Greek story of Prometheus, who snatched the thunderbolt from the hand of Jove that he might bestow upon humanity the priceless boon of fire. Verily, faith in immortality is nothing less than Promethean. It is as if mortal man, conceiving of immortality as part of the inherent life of God, had risen to the very steps of the Throne and demanded that so good a thing should not remain a divine monopoly, but that God should share it with his children.

If God is infinite, immortality is certainly not impossible; and if God is good and human immortality is really good for the moral universe, it certainly is not improbable.

The supreme contribution which the New Testament makes to the question of immortality is the person of Jesus Christ. "In Him was life; and the life was the light of men." He came that men might have life and have it more abundantly. He

190

died. What became of the material body of Jesus is not our chief concern, though no satisfactory explanation has been given of its disappearance. The tomb was empty of his body, and earth was thrilled with new life in his living presence. St. Paul said that he rose from the dead because it was not possible for death to hold Him. It would indeed appear a most astounding conclusion of such a life as that of Jesus if He had perished as a criminal and that had been the end. Life from the dead was for Him inevitable.

But "because He lives, we shall live also." Jesus tasted death for every man, that all who come to the possession of life through Him may not be obliterated by the incident of death. Our life is in Christ.

There is continuity of life in Him. Life is continuous in God, and in those who share God's life. It is a present and abiding possession. "On either side of the river was there the tree of life." It blooms and fruits both now and hereafter.

I had occasion to make a journey to California. I was returning homeward, and ascending the Rocky Mountains near the roof of the Continent.

Two engines were pulling our train, and a third was pushing behind, as we climbed toward the divide. It was a bright morning, and as we rose above the clouds we could see them huddling on the opposite side of the deep valleys. Now and then we slipped through the upper edge of one of them. For a time we rode just over the top of a cloud, and for some distance it was just below us.

There came into my section a little girl and boy who lived in Oklahoma. The boy was full of wonder and outspoken admiration. But his sister was older and worldly wise. The little boy cried:

"Oh, look! look! We're riding right on top of a cloud!"

But his sister said, "A cloud ain't nothing but fog. Nobody can't ride on a cloud; we've got rails under us, just the same as always."

The little boy said, "Jesus can ride on a cloud. I saw a picture of Him."

The little girl answered, "Yes, but that ain't us."

There are plenty of people who have that answer ready. But Jesus is "us." He is our humanity, bone of our bone and flesh of our flesh. And a

192

cloud is more than a fog. A cloud has silver linings which, for our purposes, fogs have not. A cloud can be risen above, and its upper side can be seen all lighted up by the sun.

And Jesus came into the world to show us that very nearly every good thing that is true of God may be true of us.

CHAPTER XII

CAN WE COMMUNICATE WITH THE DEAD?

A BELIEF that our loved ones are still living leads very naturally to the inquiry whether it is possible in any way to communicate with them. Attempts to establish communication with the dead are found in many forms of superstition and are not confined to the ignorant or uncivilized. The Bible affords us examples of the effort to recall the souls of those who have departed, notably in the case of Saul's visit to the Witch of Endor. The prophecies of Isaiah contain a protest against the practises of those who consult "wizards that peep and mutter" and instead exhort the seeker after knowledge to go "to the law and the testimony."

Spiritualism is a new word, but the thing for which it stands is among the oldest of human superstitions.

The belief in intercourse with the spirits of the departed in modern times may be said to begin with

Emanuel Swedenborg. This Swedish scientist and seer had trances in which he professed to speak with the mighty dead of all ages.

In the United States spiritism may be said to have begun its career of publicity in the year 1848. Two sisters, Maggie and Kate Fox, then living in Hydesville, New York, began a series of rappings, which were alleged to have been caused by supernatural means, but which in later years the sisters confessed to have been fraudulent and to have been produced by their own trickery.

Interest in spiritualism gradually diminished, until about 1890, when it seemed likely to disappear. At that time, however, the phenomena of spiritualism began to be investigated by scientific men who maintained that even the crudest and least promising phenomena of this character ought not to be ruled out as evidence until it had been carefully investigated.

Certain noted mediums became the subjects of much painstaking study by genuinely scientific men and there was organized in Great Britain and in America the Society for Psychical Research. Two of the most noted of these mediums, by reason of the attention bestowed upon them by scientific men, are Mrs. Piper of Boston, who for the past thirty years has been under almost constant supervision, and Eusapia Palladino of Naples. Eusapia was carefully studied by Cesare Lombroso of the University of Turin, who has given in detail the results of his experiment in a large book entitled, *After Death, What?* Skeptic though he was, she succeeded in convincing him. She subsequently came to America where she was detected in manifest fraud. Mrs. Piper is not known to have been engaged in consciously fraudulent performances. She has been studied by Professor William James, Professor James H. Hyslop, and other men of note. The attention given to the subject by these distinguished men gave to psychic phenomena of this general character a new dignity.*

William T. Stead, that stormy petrel of the literary world, did much to popularize this so-called science. He believed that he had learned definitely from the spirit world that he was to be kicked to

---

*Mrs. Piper's trances and alleged communications were carefully investigated by Professor G. Stanley Hall who told me that he believed her honest, but unconsciously influenced by her dependence on her seances for financial support and that he utterly discredited their supernatural character.

death by a mob, with his jaw broken by one particularly savage kick. This gave him great comfort, for he felt assured that he could die in no other way. But he went down on the *Titanic* with his jaw still in good condition.

The great World War gave to spiritualism in its various forms a new and mighty impulse. Conan Doyle having won the ear of the world with his entertaining stories of Sherlock Holmes, wrote a book, which is very dogmatic and very unconvincing, in which perhaps the best paragraphs are these, in which the spirits are alleged to elevate our thought of heaven a little above that which is given to us by the ordinary medium:

But there is a great deal of a higher intellectual life stript of grossness and materialism—the curse of the present day. Therein the inhabitants follow out their destiny much as we do here. Those who are intellectual pursue their speculations and their artistic pursuits, and every gift finds its full fruition there. Those who were less spiritual on earth remain in some intermediate state until they are ready to progress.

Heaven, as we understand it, is the final goal of all. The passing period of development varies according to the advancement or merit of the soul.

But it is strange to find persons of apparently inferior position on earth occupying there an exalted place. For the man who has worked up from humble beginnings is likely to be more highly considered than he who has had every advantage, but has been comparatively inactive throughout his life.

Nor is one's individuality merged in the new world. One is broadened, but is still tinged by the old views. The teaching of the other world is that all religions are good as long as they lead to spirituality, and are bad as far as they retard it. The man of low spiritual stature is longer traveling through to the higher plane than the other. He is isolated from contact with the best spirits, save when they descend to him upon missionary work.

There is not very much to criticize in the above, except the notion that a statement of this sort needed any intelligence for its dictation above that of Conan Doyle himself. This is simply Conan Doyle's idea of heaven and there is no reason why either he or any one else should seek to claim for it any higher authority than his own opinion. Together with the rest of his book it lacks all convincing proof of containing anything higher or nobler than he could have produced, while that which comes to him through the mediums is manifestly inferior to his own mental production.

Most notable of the products of the war as it relates to the growth of spiritualism is the book *Raymond,* by Sir Oliver Lodge. It is a memoir of his son and an account of alleged communications with him since his death.

Raymond Lodge was the youngest son of Sir Oliver and Lady Lodge. He volunteered for service in the British Army in September, 1914, received a commission as second lieutenant and was killed in action, September 14, 1915, aged twenty-six.

About six weeks before the death of Raymond, Sir Oliver received from Mrs. Piper, the noted American medium, a message purporting to have come to her from the spirit world, from his old friend, F. W. H. Myers, author in his lifetime of two massive volumes on spiritualism. The message read as follows:

"Now, Lodge . . . Myers says, you take the part of the poet, and he will act as Faunus . . . Ask Verrall; she will understand."

Sir Oliver had no difficulty in recognizing the reference to Verrall. Mrs. Verrall was a well-known spiritualist and also a classical scholar. Sir

Oliver was already a spiritualist, an active member
of the Society of Psychical Research, and for a
quarter of a century had been keenly interested in
the subject of survival after death. He made
haste to inquire of Mrs. Verrall whether she understood the allusion to Faunus. She turned to her
Horace and found a place where that poet referred
to his narrow escape from death from a falling tree.
It is a well-known passage and one sometimes
quoted in books on Latin grammar because of an
unusual grammatical construction. Horace says
that the falling of the tree might have killed him
had not Faunus, guardian of poets, preserved him.

Connington's translation of these lines reads:

"Me, the curst trunk, that smote my skull,
Had slain; but Faunus, strong to shield
The friends of Mercury, check'd the blow
In mid descent."

Mrs. Piper received this communication August
8, 1915, and mailed it to Sir Oliver. He wrote to
Mrs. Verrall and she answered him on September
8, citing the above text and translation. It would be
interesting to know just what impression Sir Oliver
got from it when he first received this interpreta-

tion. Apparently Mrs. Verrall guessed correctly the meaning of Mrs. Piper's allusion. It is not necessary to suppose that Mrs. Piper received any supernatural information concerning Faunus, nor was it necessary for her to become a classical scholar. In her rather wide and superficial reading she could quite easily have fallen upon the passage. No great risk was run in sending it to Sir Oliver. Assuming that his studies in other lines had caused him to ignore the passage, it was a safe guess that Mrs. Verrall would be able to identify the reference. If after that nothing happened to Sir Oliver it was because his friend Myers was doing for him what Faunus did for Horace. If anything terrible happened it would be safe to assume that it would have been worse but for the protection of Myers still acting the part of Faunus, defender of the friends of Mercury. Sir Oliver Lodge is no poet and the allusion was rather far-fetched. But it answered all the requirements.

It is interesting to note, however, that Myers, who was a noted spiritualist in his day and master of all the arts of that system, being now in heaven, was compelled to send his messages to his old friend, equally skilled in matters of spiritualism, by way of Mrs. Piper and by further way of Mrs. Verrall. Far-fetched and ambiguous and round-about as the message was, it is the only thing in the book possessing any approach to inherent dignity. The Delphic oracle was not more ambiguous. The Faunus message if never interpreted did no harm, and if interpreted it was certain to be a satisfaction to a man like Sir Oliver Lodge, whether anything happened or not.

Six days after Sir Oliver received Mrs. Verrall's interpretation of Mrs. Piper's transmitted message from Mr. Myers, Second Lieutenant Raymond Lodge was killed in action. His death occurred on September fourteenth and the family soon learned of it. Sir Oliver and Lady Lodge lost little time in going to a professional medium. A Mrs. Kennedy, who had lost a son in June of the same year and had introduced herself to Sir Oliver Lodge by letter on August sixteenth, proffered her good offices as soon as she knew of the death of Raymond and arranged for very nearly all the sittings that followed in which Sir Oliver and his wife consulted professional mediums and obtained what they thought were revelations. Lady Lodge went on the twenty-fifth of September, and Sir Oliver hurried to London two days later to see the same medium, a Mrs. Leonard. This Mrs. Leonard had as her control a little Indian maiden named Feda, and talked a sort of foolish baby-talk, pronouncing Raymond, "Yaymond" and she wiggled her own body to show how Raymond's dog wagged its tail in heaven.

We shall not follow Sir Oliver and Lady Lodge on their weary and credulous tramp from one medium to another. The story from this time on is the drivel of a medium under the alleged control of Feda, the Indian child, Moonstone a dead Yogi, Biddy an Irish washer-woman, and other puerile or senile personalities of the spirit world. The details may be read in full in Sir Oliver's book and they are pathetic in their vapidity.

The first message came to Mrs. Kennedy from her own son through a professional medium. It read:

"I have seen that boy, Sir Oliver's son; he's better, and has a splendid rest. Tell his people."

Perhaps in the spirit land a lad of seventeen

speaks of a man of twenty-six and a commissioned officer as "that boy." But that is not the custom in the British army; indeed, the activity of Mrs. Kennedy in these subsequent sittings with professional mediums opens every necessary opportunity for such information as a medium requires. Sir Oliver states he believes that Mrs Kennedy did not give the medium any information as to who were the distinguished visitors coming to them; and he says it is not probable that mediums have time to hunt up family information. Both suppositions are distinctly contrary to probability. Indeed, when it was known that a son of Sir Oliver Lodge had been killed, every medium in London must have been on tiptoe with expectation that he and his family would be seeking communication with Raymond. The newspapers must have furnished them a considerable part of the information they wanted and Mrs. Kennedy may at least have dropped a few unintentional intimations that the people for whom she was arranging sittings were very important people.

Sir Oliver and Lady Lodge obtained what they wanted. They secured communications from Raymond and a detailed description of the dog he had with him in heaven, the dog who according to Feda had nice hair and seemed to be of dark color and had ears that did not stand up and that wagged his tail in a manner which Feda illustrated by body movements of her own. Beside this description of Raymond's dog, the most interesting things communicated by Raymond Lodge and Paul Kennedy, were, first, that heaven is filled with the lonely souls of dead soldiers, eager to communicate with their friends but unable to do so unless those friends will consult professional mediums; and secondly, (Sir Oliver Lodge appeared to count this a sort of scientific basis for the continuity of substance and life in heaven) that things rotting here on earth send up a stench which affords the physical basis for their restoration as actual entities in heaven. This is a heaven made up out of the bad smells of earth, a place of celestial stenches, glorified and made immortal!

There is one other bit of alleged evidence which he introduces, namely, a reference to a photograph of Raymond, which the family did not know to be in existence, a group photograph which later came to them. Considering, however, how busy the camera was in making group photographs of soldiers, it would have been almost miraculous if some such group had not contained a picture of Raymond. The photograph is published in the book and very nearly every detail of it appears to have been incorrectly reported by the medium.

What most impresses a reader is the utter lack of anything that can truthfully be called the scientific spirit in the book. Sir Oliver Lodge is, or has been, a great scientist, but this is neither a great book nor a scientific book. The author's fame as a scientist can not protect him from the just criticism of having given to the world as spiritual comfort the drivel of the ignorant and designing medium.

The grief of a heart-broken father entitles Sir Oliver Lodge to the reader's sincere sympathy; but neither this nor any awe of his great name can protect him from the righteous indignation of those who resent this foisting upon the world of so-called comfort in the form of a heaven with cigars and whisky and soda and of utterly vapid occupations and concerns. Perhaps the most comforting thing that Sir Oliver and Mrs. Lodge might have got would have been the description of Raymond's dog, which, unfortunately they were not able to identify.

He has brought that doggie again, nice doggie. A doggie that goes like this, and twists about (Feda indicating a wriggle). He has got a nice tail, not a little stumpy tail, nice tail with nice hair on it. He sits up like that sometimes, and comes down again, and puts his tongue out of his mouth. He's got a cat, too, plenty of animals, he says. He hasn't seen any lions and tigers, but he has seen horses, cats, dogs, and birds. He says you know this doggie, he has nice hair, a little wavy, which sticks up all over him, and has twists at the end. Now he's jumping round. He hasn't got a very pointed face, but it isn't like a little pug-dog either; it's rather a long shape. And he has nice ears with flaps not standing up; nice long hairs on them too, darkish color he looks, darkish, as near as I can see him.

To such low estate has science fallen in Sir Oliver Lodge's investigation that the evidence which he submits contains all the crudities and vulgarities of the trance-medium, the table-rapper and the automatic writer. By these several methods, each with its invitation to fraud and its necessity of employing professional interpreters of alleged spirit messages, he and his family are supposed to have communicated with his dead son. All Sir Oliver Lodge's twenty-five years of work in the Society of Psychical Research had not availed to make it possible for Raymond to come to his father directly. All his dead associates in the Society of Psychical Research, including Mr. Myers, were helpless to come to him, except through these crude and suspicious agencies. It is interesting to read that at one of these seances a table which had been rapping out Raymond's messages became so charged with Raymond's living personality that it tried to climb up into Lady Lodge's lap.

Sir Oliver Lodge himself in an interview a few months after the publication of his book, admitted that no progress had been made in subsequent revelation. He said:

"The stress and anxiety to communicate have subsided in our case. The wish to give evidence remains, but now that the fact of survival and happy employment is established, the communications are placid."

The happy employment referred to would appear to be chiefly the use of cigars and whisky and soda and playing with the dog which Feda described with characteristic ambiguity. If Sir Oliver and his family are comforted, no one else need complain.

Professor James H. Hyslop in his book, *Life after Death,* approaches the phenomena of the professional mediums in a much more scientific spirit than Sir Oliver Lodge. He admits the crudity and vulgarities of the mediums, and he urges that the intellectual limitations of the medium, the inadequacy of language to convey meanings except in terms of the sensory life and the pragmatic nature of the ordinary mind, carry with them an almost irresistible tendency to conceive of any spiritual environment after the analogy of the physical world.

This is the best explanation that can probably be given and it is entitled to some weight. Hyslop says:

The spiritual life after death is mentally created, so to speak, and hence the analogies with the earthly life are not sensory in respect to stimulus, but mental and creative. That is to say, it is not the physical life that survives, but the inner life and death leaves us with the internal mental

209

faculties intact. The spirit enters into the new life with memory, imagination and self-consciousness; and it builds up an idealistic world in the new state of existence formed according to our degree of progress in spiritual things, and more or less a reflection of our earthly experience.

He, therefore, maintains that there is a three-fold limitation. The spirit itself is limited in its new environment. The medium is limited in powers of interpretation. We also are limited in respect to that which we are able to receive from the spirit world.

Accepting this statement by Professor Hyslop as reasonable, two questions arise. First, why is it that with heaven filled with spirits in all grades of spiritual development, virtually the only ones which have succeeded in establishing communication with earth are those who talk baby talk, or who jabber in foolish, broken sentences? Why must Raymond, in looking about heaven for some one to convey a message to his father, communicate through the little Indian maiden Feda, whose Indian chatter appears as such only to those who never knew any Indians? Why must he go to the spirit of Moonstone, the dead Yogi, or to the soul

210

of Biddy, the Irish washer-woman? Why do none
of Oliver Lodge's associates in the Society of Psychical Research talk to him in language at least as
good as they were accustomed to use when on
earth?

A few years ago a St. Louis woman undertook
to interest her friends in some alleged communications which she professed to have had from a lady
of about the Elizabethan period who discoursed in
alleged old English and claimed the name of Patience Worth. Her literary achievements interested some people who should have known better,
and resulted in the publication of a volume of the
writings alleged to have been of this person. The
volume presumably may still be found by any who
care to see what mediocre performances the spirits indulge in and how highly these banalities are
rated by those who bring to them the proper quality of adoration. As a matter of fact, no single
great thought has come into human life through
any modern commerce with alleged spirits. The
souls of the mighty dead have shriveled pitifully
if they are now capable of such trash as the mediums have uttered in their name.

Agnes Repplier in a magazine article, entitled

Dead Authors, makes a rather long list of people who were able to write good literature when they were on earth, from whom alleged revelations have recently been received, and neither Mark Twain nor O. Henry nor Charles Dickens is now able to write anything nearly as good as when he was on earth.

The other question relates to the intellectual and spiritual caliber of the medium. Even Mrs. Piper, most famous of American mediums, had as her habitual "control" a queerly named spirit less intelligent than herself. Professor William James, who studied her for twenty years, had to admit that he awaited "new facts, clearer and more precise" before he could say with certainty whether her alleged revelations contained anything of the supernatural. He died waiting. Meantime her powers of this character instead of growing more brilliant have diminished.

It might be supposed, because alleged spiritistic phenomena come to us now vouched for by noted men of science, that there has been some change in their character since the table-rapping of the Fox sisters and the crude and illiterate babblings of the mediums. On the contrary, we are still face to face with the familiar old methods, which 'lent themselves so easily to fraud that they were exposed as such in case after case. The only notable difference is that now these are the alleged phenomena of the spirit world under scientific observation. Now we have the phenomena catalogued and the alleged communications recorded, and the means of fraud lessened if not eliminated. But the means of fraud were not eliminated in the case of Eusapia Palladino, who interested the scientific investigators of two continents, and who completely deceived even so seasoned a skeptic as Lombroso.

The most recent notable case in America of alleged spirit communication under conditions which entitle it to any attention is that of "Margery" the wife of a prominent Boston surgeon. Her case has been the subject of investigation at Harvard, under a commission appointed by the *Scientific American,* which has offered a prize for a well authenticated super-normal revelation under test conditions. Full accounts of this case have been published. The interesting fact is, not that the case is manifestly one where deliberate imposture has been practised, but that such imposture, of the crudest possible sort, so nearly succeeded in imposing upon the learned men who observed the case.*

When those who profess to come to us with revelations from the dead begin by surrounding themselves with apparatus such as might easily lend itself to fraud, and such as repeatedly has been used in the interests of fraud, it begins to be time for sensible people to lose interest.

People who read the names of the distinguished men who have surrendered to this delusion, do not all consider that the revelations which they suppose themselves to have received are not direct revelations to themselves, but such revelations as they have been able to delude themselves into supposing they have received through mediums, not all of them of very high intellectual or moral grade, and through such experiences as the attempt of a table to climb up into the lap of Lady Lodge and cuddle there as a substitute for the grown man who had once been her baby, and who had died an officer on the battle-field.

---

*See concerning this investigation an article on "Science and the Medium" by Hudson Hoagland, in the *Atlantic Monthly*, for November, 1925.

This at least deserves to be remembered concerning all this recent interest in spiritualism, that it does not appear to have in it a shred of religion. When Conan Doyle affirms that in this form religion is to survive, he seems to fail to inquire whether the form of belief which he is commending is in any true sense religious. Life after death is not of necessity religious, any more than life before death is religious. A heaven of woolly dogs and whisky and soda is not of necessity religious. What has been disclosed in all this alleged revelation concerning God, or love or hope or duty?

Is it any comfort to believe that our beloved dead are occupied in nothing better worth while than in trying to "get across" with such communications as have come from the tipped tables and the dark cabinet and the alleged trance utterance of the mediums?

Meantime, those men and women who earn their money by making people think they have news from heaven have awaiting them a standing reward when they can exhibit any proof that the phenomena they produce require belief in a supernatural agency, or can not be duplicated by clever magicians. Until we have some better evidence than yet has come to us it is better and more dignified and more religious to leave our beloved who have departed beyond our sight in the hands of the Father of their spirits and ours.

My own mother died more than thirty-five years ago. She was an earnest, spiritually minded woman, who had implicit faith in immortality, and if there is such a thing as communication between the two worlds, her spirit could have no greater joy than in communication with the children whom she dearly loved. Let us suppose then that my mother desires to send a message to me. What will be the process by which she establishes communication with her eldest son?

In the first place she will be compelled to look about heaven until she finds some little Indian maiden, or some Irish washer-woman who is on speaking terms with some particular medium; then Feda or Biddy will communicate with me through some woman, whom my mother, if living, would be very desirous that I should not know. Then with my mother's beautiful thoughts vulgarized into alleged Indian baby talk by Feda and still further vulgarized by the medium, I may obtain some precious piece of information which it is supposed the medium could not have known and which therefore the spirit of my mother must have communicated.

What will that message be? This perhaps, or something as important, that there is a small hole in the toe of my left stocking caused by a nail in my shoe of which up to the present time I have had no knowledge. If having paid two dollars to the medium I return home and find the hole and the nail I am supposed to admit that this must have been a message from my mother in heaven. It is my own opinion that if my mother in heaven ever sends a message to me she will send it through some channel that she would have recognized while living and that the message itself will possess inherent value.

We have need of a revival of faith in immortality without superstition. We need a heaven high above the maudlin and almost imbecile heaven of the mediums. We need a life beyond the grave which is worthy of God, the author of life, and of Jesus Christ, who brought life and immortality to light.

It is not enough to believe that our dead friends exist in a state of celestial feeble-mindedness, and that we may communicate with them through persons admittedly their intellectual and spiritual inferiors upon this side. We need faith in an immortality that possesses ethical and spiritual value.

Jesus said, "Lay hold on eternal life." The word "eternal" as He used it had more than the suggestion of time: it had in it the connotation of a moral value. His words meant "Lay hold on the life that is life indeed." The doctrine of life after death as Jesus taught it is more than the doctrine of the continuity of existence. It is the doctrine of the permanence of spiritual values. Such a doctrine, the doctrine of a life beyond the grave based upon the integrity of God, the value of moral life, and the deepest and most ennobling affirmations of the human intellect, and the richest and most abiding longings of the human soul, is the doctrine that in the present hour of spiritual chaos needs to be uttered with assurance and power.

Nor need we question the practical value of such a faith. It will impart value to this present life, and give added worth to every article of Christian faith. "Godliness is profitable unto all things, having promise of the life that now is, and that which is to come." Every effort to make this a better world will be mightily strengthened by a renewed faith that this life is a part of God's great whole. The social gospel needs for its higher reaches of endeavor and the crown of its aspiration and the motive of its activity this dynamic which is attested in the Word of God—"the power of an endless life."

Are our dead friends near us, and do they know what we are doing, and can they share our life and thought?

I hope they do not know all that causes us anxiety and concern. If they do, I hope they are enough wiser than we not to fret and worry as we do. I hope that the veil between us is sufficiently merciful to shut from their sight some of our follies and sins and pains. But I should not like to think that they had no part in our life and no knowledge of how it fares with us.

I have sometimes thought of it in this way. Let us suppose that the spirits of our loved ones, more on the other side than here, still have a community of interest, still cherish a common concern for our well-being, yet are unable to communicate with us. Would that be so very lonely and unnatural an experience? We have an analogy in our present life. It is the family concern for the baby not yet born.

Consider for a moment a home in which there is to be a baby. The father and mother know about it, have known for a long time. Even the children are told that before very long God will send to this home a little life, a new little brother or sister. The whole family shares the knowledge of the little one that is to be born.

Now, this little unborn life is not up in heaven, nor on another planet, nor far away. It is here, among us, under the same roof with us. Mother is carrying this precious little life under her heart until the glad and solemn day when through the blessed and awful ministry of pain it shall be born. It is no stranger to be sent to us from a foreign land; it is already a member of the family, here just as certainly as we are here.

We can influence this little life already. In countless ways we can make provision for it. We can love it, and we do; we can pray for it, and we do. When it comes, it is not an intrusion; it is the manifestation of a life that all the while had been among us.

I do not know any reason why it may not be so in the case of our loved ones who have been born into the heavenly life. There is no reason for us to think of them as distant; they may not be remote at all. They may be as conscious of us as we were conscious of the unborn child. They may love us, care for us, and promote our welfare in ways we do not know.

Life would be poor but for our dead. They are still ours. They are not hopelessly lost to us. And they may be nearer to us than we think.

CHAPTER XIII

UNTO THE NETHERMOST

I AM ready now to meet the objection of some reader who may have followed the argument thus far, but has held all the while in the back of his mind a serious objection. He says, if I hear him aright, "It would be very pleasant to agree with you, but your faith in immortality has joined to it a terrible corollary. You believe in an eternal hell, into which those who leave this world in what you call sin are plunged in hopeless and unspeakable torment. I have had friends, well-loved and dear to me, who left this world in the state you thus describe. I can not pretend that they were Christians; I can not even say that they were good. But they were not hopeless, even as judged by our short measure of hope. No human father, no matter how sorely tried and perplexed with their folly and perverseness, would have sent them even to prison,

222

much less to hell. You have made the doctrine of immortality, which ought to have been beautiful, a very terrible thing on account of your teaching of eternal retribution. I would far rather believe that God wiped the slate clean, got rid of all of us, charged up our virtues to profit and our sins to loss, than to believe in an eternal hell."

I am ready, as I have said, to face this objection, which I think has right to a frank consideration.

The doctrine of an endless hell, flaming with physical torture, may be said to have been a very precious one in the past, and in some form a very necessary one. But we shudder as we look back no very long time to what good people thought they believed about it. No gentler soul lived than Isaac Watts, yet what terrible things he put into some of his hymns, of people doomed to endless death, yet never dying, and this for the primary reason that they had inherited the sin of Adam:

Backward with humble Shame we look
   On our Original;
How is our Nature dashed and broke
   In our first Father's Fall!

How strong in our degenerate Blood
   The old Corruption reigns,

And mingling with the crooked Flood
Wanders through all our Veins!

Here is another hymn which our ancestors loved
to sing:

Far in the Deep where Darkness dwells
The Land of Horror and Despair,
Justice has built a dismal hell,
And laid her stores of Vengeance there.

Eternal Plagues and heavy chains,
Tormenting Racks, and fiery Coals,
And darts to inflict immortal Pains,
Dyed in the Blood of damnèd Souls.

There Satan, the first Sinner, lies,
And roars, and bites his Iron Bands;
In vain the Rebel strives to rise,
Crushed with the weight of both Thy hands.

There guilty Ghosts of Adam's Race
Shriek out, and howl beneath Thy rod;
Once they could scorn a Saviour's grace,
But they incensed a dreadful God.

Tremble, my soul, and kiss the Son,
Sinner, obey the Saviour's Call,
Else your Damnation hastens on,
And Hell gapes wide to wait your Fall.

This is the terrible picture of the God of their hymns:

> His Nostrils breathe out fiery Streams,
>   And from his awful Tongue
> A sovereign Voice divides the Flames
>   And Thunder roars along.
>
> Tempests of angry Fire shall roll
>   To blast the Rebel Worm,
> And beat upon his naked soul
>   In one eternal Storm.

This is the picture of the living death to which a loving God was supposed to have consigned his children:

> What, to be banished from my Life,
>   And yet forbid to die:
> To linger in eternal Pain,
>   Yet death forever fly?

It is possible that there are still some Christians, and very gentle ones, who hold these views; but these dogmas no longer appear in our hymn-books. He who believes in this kind of a hell must believe it alone; he can not find others to sing it with him, nor a hymn-book in which it is set to be sung.

I believe in hell. If there is no hell, it is time one was established. If there is no hell, some one has been negligent.

But there is a hell. I have seen men in it. Furthermore, I have known men living who have made no visible preparation here for any other kind of future. I have known men who, if they lived afterward as they lived here, were of such sort that, if they died and did not find a hell, they would have established one within fifteen minutes after their arrival in heaven. Character being what it is, some sort of hell is inevitable. The Bible teaches that there is a hell. And the Bible does not describe it as a desirable place. The figures of speech which are used to describe it are most unpleasant.

But what is the character of hell? Is it a place for the display of the divine vindictiveness? Is it a place where sin is licensed to go on forever unrestrained? Is it a place where God has abdicated, and where love can never enter? So far as that part of the universe is concerned, has God given it up in despair?

I could not believe any of those things if I believed as I do in a good God. If there is a hell, and

226

I think there is, men make it themselves by their own wickedness; it is the inevitable expression of their own character.

If there is a hell, it is a good hell. A good God could permit no other kind. If there is a hell, a good God has established it because it is the logical and necessary result of character expressing itself in destiny. If there is a hell it is because the moral universe needs it. I will go even further and say that if there is a hell, it is because those who go there need it. If there is a hell it is because it is the best place to which a loving God can send, or permit to be sent, the people whose own wilfulness drives them in violation of God's desire that they would accept something better. I think there is such a hell.

Let us frankly admit that the Hebrew word which is translated "hell" conveyed no such meaning to the Jewish mind as our English word "hell" conveys to present-day readers. "Sheol" was not primarily a place of torture, but the abode of the dead. Sometimes it was thought of as divided, but the division had no such sharp and clear definition as has come to it in Christian theology.

Our modern word hell conveys to the imagination a very different thought than that which it brought to the people of the Old Testament. When the Psalmist said, "If I make my bed in Sheol," he did not think of a place of torment as a punishment for sin. He was thinking of some dark, gloomy and forbidding abode of the dead, a place shrouded with gloom and impenetrable to human investigation. He was thinking of the place to which all human life goes and from which no human life returns.

The Psalmist asked himself whether the abode of the dead was a place of utter hopelessness. He thought it could not be so. No barrier could shut God out of there. Life and death were not to him so absolutely inseparable that God could be shut out from any part of his universe.

This was what the Psalmist was thinking and in strict justice to his thought we ought to use the word "Sheol" here instead of the word "hell." Yet, I am using the word "hell" with intent, for if the Psalmist's thought is true at all, it must be true not only of the Hebrew Sheol but of the Christian's hell. There can not be any part of God's moral universe from which God himself is excluded. The Love that dwells in the highest heaven must somehow reach to the lowest hell.

I am willing to ask whether even with our bluntest and cruelest modern conception attaching to the word "hell," the verse is not true? Is God in the bottomless pit? There are verses in the Bible which read as if that might be true. The wicked are spoken of as banished from the presence of God. Yet I must believe for myself that banishment from God's presence can only be a fact of experience and not of actual reality. To say of a sinner that he departs from the presence of God is the same as to say the sun goes down. But the sun does nothing of the sort: the earth merely turns its back upon the sun and hides in the darkness of its own shadow. The sun is shining all the time: the earth can not possibly get out of the sunshine. All it can do is to make a little tapering shadow and creep into it, but that shadow is less than a flyspeck on the face of the heavens. The sun is flooding the universe with light. Even the light which the earth stops by casting a shadow is not destroyed. It is gathered up on the face which the earth exposes to the sun and not a ray of all that glorious light is permanently wasted.

God himself must be in hell. It is a shocking thing to say, but it certainly must be true. If it were not so God would be less than infinite. There can be no corner of God's universe from which He is absent. The sufferings of the damned are not apart from Him, they are not unfelt by Him. In the last analysis I think they are not inflicted by Him. They inhere in the very nature of sin, which makes it inevitable that transgression should carry with it shame and pain.

Shall we say that the sufferings of hell are redemptive? I should not dare to say that because I do not know. There is nothing in the Bible that forbids that hope. I will not argue with any one about the mere meaning of the Greek and Hebrew words. It is not on the basis of the definition of single words that great doctrines like this are to be established. We can not be sure enough that we know the precise meaning of any ancient word in any dead language to determine on that basis alone our theory of hope for eternity. Somehow, sometime, God will manifest his kindness even in the blackness of the bottomless pit. There is no blackness anywhere that is not somehow spanned by the rainbow of his goodness and his hope.

Jesus spent most of his life in villages. When He visited Jerusalem He was interested in many of the details in which city life differed from rural and village life. One of these was the disposal of sewage and garbage. That is a problem in every city and always has been. Jerusalem met the problem in the crude but reasonably effective method of the age. It carted its refuse to the valley of Gehenna and there burned what could be burned and left the rest to decompose on a level considerably lower than that of the city's water supply. Jesus used Jerusalem's city dump as a figure of speech for God's method of dealing with refractory material. He said it would have to be thrown out into the valley of Gehenna "where the worm dieth not and the fire is not quenched."

This figurative use of Jerusalem's dump has done much to define the popular idea of hell, and its very name, "Gehenna," is preserved in the translation: for "Sheol" in the Old Testament and "hades" in the New, ought never to be translated "hell." Let us recall for a moment the Jerusalem garbage pile, and the method of sewage disposal.

The undying worm and the unquenchable fire are not symbols of torture, but of conservation. They are the symbols of the utilization of waste. The worm does not die, not because any one maggot is miraculously endowed with immortality, but because the dump wagons are continually carting in more material for worms to feed upon and to lay eggs in. It is not because any one worm continues to gnaw, or because any one carcass survives to be gnawed.

The fire is not quenched because more fuel is continuously added. It is not because any one scrap of waste paper continues forever to burn. So far as the Jerusalem dump is concerned, when fuel ceases to be carted there will be no more devouring worm, and no more unquenchable fire.

Meantime, the unquenched fire takes filth and makes of it clean ashes, good fertilizer, or even if leeched, good antiseptic. And the worm, ugly as he is to look at, converts garbage into something less repulsive. Then a bird flies over the valley and eats the worm; and the carrion becomes a carol;

the stench is transformed into a song. Even the worm and the fire are God's beneficent agents for turning the elements of destruction into products of constructive value to the world. They are not the symbols of despair but of God's apparently thwarted but ultimately triumphant hope.

Something should be said about the day of Judgment. There is such a day, and every day is a Judgment day. But "God hath appointed a day in which He will judge the world in righteousness, by that Man whom He hath ordained," the Lord Jesus Christ. It is no less comforting than alarming to know that there is to be a future reckoning; and it is most significant that both here and elsewhere Jesus the Christ is declared to furnish the basis of Judgment.

The Fourth Gospel has this interesting word about the day of Judgment and the Judge:

"For neither doth the Father judge any man, but He hath given all judgment unto the son; . . . And he gave him authority to execute judgment, because he is a son of man."—John 5:22-27.

If you read these verses in the American Revision you will see that the word "son" in the title

233

"Son of man" is not capitalized as it usually is in the New Testament. That of course represents the judgment of the translators and might be a mistake, but if you will read the passage carefully in the trend and meaning of Jesus' argument, you will be likely to conclude that the translators are correct. The King James Version was unquestionably wrong in using the definite article. When Jesus called himself "the Son of Man" He used the title in a sense that involved a particular distinction, but when He says that God, the Father, judges no man but has committed all judgment unto the son, "because he is a son of man," the term has a very different connotation. The Twentieth Century Version thus translates it. "Indeed the Father does not judge any one, but has entrusted the work of judging entirely to his Son; . . . and because He is man He has also given Him authority to act as judge."

We must not lose any part of the force of this affirmation. It affirms distinctly that were Jesus divine and only divine He would have some measure of disqualification for acting as the world's final judge. The Father judgeth no man, but His Son being man will be their judge.

234

This does not imply that the judgment will be a light thing for the wilfully wicked; but it promises that its tests will be reasonable and sympathetic, and its standards adjusted to human values and motives.

His sympathy will not be the only quality in which the humanity of Jesus will fit Him to be our judge. Just because He was human, but in his humanity realized and lived the life of divinity, He must judge us for any failure we have made to attain that measure of divineness which was possible to us. "Of his fulness have all we received" and there was grace to supersede all grace which we thus far have realized and more than we have appropriated. For this failure we must be judged, not by the standards of an impossible Omnipotence but by the measure of those qualities realized in the human life of Jesus. He met temptation and successfully resisted it and called for no miracle to be wrought to enable Him thus to overcome. He lived and loved and died with the life of God triumphant in his mortal flesh. Have we done the same?

Hope is the Cinderella of the three Christian

235

graces. Faith and love are appraised at their real
value, but hope is hopelessly at a disadvantage between them. Faith is a condition of salvation, and
love is salvation. What room have we for hope?
The answer is, that hope is the dynamic of salvation. The epistle to the Hebrews tells us that hope
is an anchor to the soul (Hebrews 6:19). So it is,
and the anchor is its emblem, but hope is more than
an anchor; it is an engine.

Glorious things are said of hope by artists and
poets, but after all most of them pity hope and say
of her, "Poor thing; it's fortunate she doesn't know
what really is coming." Thousands of people look
at Watt's familiar painting and say, "Is that
Hope? I should think that was Despair." The
poets indeed have made Hope and Despair twin
sisters. Milton says in *Paradise Lost*:

What reinforcement we may gain from hope:
If not what resolution from despair.

Shelley went further and said,

Worse than despair,
Worse than the bitterness of death, is hope.

Others who do not go so far are never able to

236

think of hope without remembering how little there is to hope for.

Shakespeare tells us that

> The miserable have no other medicine,
>   But only hope.

Pope in his Essay on Man, tells us that

> Hope springs eternal in the human breast:
> Man never *is,* but always *to be* blest.

Through all these and a multitude of other quotations runs this idea that it is rather desirable that men should hope, but that there is not very much to hope for. It is thus we discount one of the three abiding Christian virtues.

Greek mythology had its story of the creation of man. To Prometheus and his brother Epimetheus was committed this task. Epimetheus had distributed the gifts of life so lavishly to others that he had very little left to give to man; and for his sake Prometheus ascending to heaven brought down the gift of fire. To punish him for his audacity, Prometheus was chained to the rock with vultures forever tearing at his vitals, while to Epimetheus was sent the curse of the first woman. Her name was Pandora, for every one of the gods had given something to make her, and she had a box containing all the curses and just one blessing. Being charged by her husband never to open the box, she lifted the cover with no worse intent than to take a momentary peep within, but all the ills of humanity, both those that afflict men's bodies and those that torment the mind, rushed out. She shut the cover down barely in time to retain the one blessing, and that was hope. It was a poor compensation for the ill she had done, but it was richly worth the saving.

Hope is among the most precious of human assets. We belittle it. We discount it. We count it a mark of inexperience. We say, "Blessed are they who expect nothing," that is who have ceased to hope, "for they shall never be disappointed." On the contrary, we ought to say, Blessed are they who, no matter how often they are disappointed, steadfastly continue to hope for all that is good.

Alexander the Great wept because there were no more worlds to conquer. That is not surprising. He was still a young man, and conquest was the business of kings. Any of us might do the same if we saw the end of life completely attained and the long years stretching ahead with nothing left to kindle the imagination or nerve the arm to valiant endeavor.

I remember reading of a young American business man who had attained early in life everything he had thought desirable, and it had all come to him easily. Education, business success, wealth and social standing were all his; and one night a company gathered in his honor to congratulate him on the completeness of his success. He received all the congratulations of his friends, and that night went home and put a bullet through his brain.

Not without reason have the poets and philosophers linked together those two contrasting elements, despair and hope. Even despair could not produce quite the paralysis of hope rendered hopeless by complete achievement.

The World War raised anew the question whether we have a right to hope for salvation after death for those whom we do not know to have accepted Christ in this life. Our country suffered so little in comparison with Great Britain and the nations of the continent, we can hardly realize how tremendous has been the pressure of this appeal to those who hold the Christian faith and who have lost loved ones that had given no indication in their lifetime of their personal acceptance of Christ as a Saviour. In less degree, but still insistently, the question comes up to Christian thinkers here, "Are we forbidden to hope that our loved ones are saved?"

I have an unqualified answer to this question. We are not forbidden to hope for any good thing, for ourselves or for those dear to us.

A while ago I had occasion to attend a portion of a murder trial. The defendant was a woman, and the circumstances were such that it was important that she should establish a reputation for previous good character. One of the witnesses who appeared on her behalf was a neighbor and friend, and the attorney for the prosecution asked her on cross-examination a series of questions intending to show that she was not an unprejudiced witness. He asked her in succession, "Are you near neighbors? Are you intimate friends?" To these and other like questions she answered affirmatively.

Then he asked her, "Do you not hope that she is going to be acquitted?" "I object," interrupted the attorney for the defense, and then, very quietly, he added, "We all hope she is going to be acquitted."

The judge sustained the objection. It was the duty of every member of the jury to hope that she would be acquitted and to find her not guilty if he could.

Our criminal jurisprudence compels judge and jury to hope for the acquittal of the accused and to give him the benefit of every reasonable doubt.

Orthodox preaching has constantly reminded itself that it must not take the edge off its appeal to men by holding out a hope of pardon after death. That feeling has been justified. We have no right to be dogmatic at a point where the word of God is so reticent, nor have we any right to superimpose our hard and fast meanings upon Scripture terms which were never intended thus to be employed.

As Joseph Cook used to say with such tremendous emphasis, we have no right to teach men that it is safe for them to die in their sins. It certainly is not safe for men so to die. Neither is it safe for them to live in their sins.

241

There is an old story of a devout old lady who rose in prayer meeting and said, "Lord, thou knowest that some people teach that all men are going to heaven; but we hope for something better than that." We should all be able to say, Amen, to such a prayer. I, personally, hope that God will find some way of making men fit for heaven; and that is something better than simply that they should get there.

Of this I am sure. Punishment for sin will not continue after it ceases to do good. God's love and mercy are not limited to time but belong also to eternity. If God does not save men in the next world it will be for the same reason that God does not save some men here, namely, that after God has done his utmost those men refuse to be saved.

I have said that I dare to hope that God's infinite love and compassion reach far beyond the limits of this short life. I believe that if God does not save men in the future life, it will be for the same reason that He does not save all men here, namely that they wilfully resist his salvation, so that He can not save them with a salvation which is of their free choice. I do not dogmatize on a theme so obscure, but I shall not be less than completely honest when I say that I hope that there is no eternity of suffering and sin. I hope that God has some better way of dealing with even the worst of human sinners than to keep them alive that they may sin eternally and thus compel Him to punish them eternally. When sin stops, then, I think, punishment will stop; and I hope that sin will not go on forever.

An English poet, J. E. Flecker, has written a short poem called *Tenebris Interlucentem,* in which he suggests how even in hell some gracious influence from without might stir a generous impulse within. If so, God will not refuse to send it.

> A linnet who had lost her way
> Sang on a blackened bough in Hell,
> Till all the ghosts remembered well
> The trees, the wind, the golden day.
>
> At last they knew that they had died,
> When they heard music in that land;
> And some one there stole forth a hand
> To draw a brother to his side.

Some good people, accepting as Bible truth the doctrines which they had heard preached concerning hell, have suffered exquisite and unmerited tortures by reason of the death of loved ones whom they could not honestly declare were Christians, but whom they loved too much, and found too lovable, to believe that they deserved to be damned. Yet for these who were dearer to them than life they knew no possible fate but the eternal fires of satanic retribution. If this book shall fall into the hands of any such person, a father, perhaps or mother, to whom the grief had been hard enough without this excruciating element of cruel torture, let me say a word of comfort.

I did not know this boy or girl or friend of yours, and have no authority to say what judgment awaits upon the other shore. But this I know, your love for this dear one is less than God's, and his compassion is greater than yours. If there is anything that your love could do for that loved one, be sure God's love will not do less. "If ye, then, being evil," can not reconcile your thought to this dear one's eternal loss, "how much more shall your Father who is in heaven" find methods of expressing a love that is not willing any should perish.

Does any one say, "I thought you were an orthodox minister, and I discover that you are a Universalist?" I am an orthodox minister, and I do not belong to the denomination which bears the fine name of Universalist. I am not sure that I am in all points in agreement with them, and I am abundantly happy in my own church. I once heard a Universalist minister say he believed "that God's patch would be as large as sin's rent." I should not be willing to believe less. I believe more. I do not believe that where sin abounds grace shall almost as much abound, but that where sin abounds grace shall much more abound. I have some hope that I shall be found to cherish a belief almost as large as the promises of God and the love of Jesus Christ. That love can save to the uttermost.

I hope. I hope for every sweet and beautiful thing I can think of. I hope there will not be an eternity of sin and suffering. I hope that sin will some time have run its mad course, and God will be all in all. I hope God will not maintain forever a protected and segregated red-light district. I should be ashamed of myself if I did not hope for something better than that sin and shame and suffering would go on forever. I hope the devil will either die or be converted. I dare not hope for anything less.

I do not pretend to know; I only hope. And yet some things I think I know. I know that so long as hell endures, God suffers. I know that so long as there is one lost soul, Christ is on the cross. I hope for entirety, unity, and all-pervading goodness. I hope this because I know that God is good. Hell will not endure forever unless such eternity is necessary to the expression of divine love.

There are two arguments used by good men which do not in the least appeal to me. One of them is this. Jesus said that the wicked shall go into eternal punishment, and the word *aionios* in the Greek means eternal and nothing else. That argument does not convince me; it does not even touch me. No modern lexicon can tell us precisely the meaning of any word in a dead language. We can not be sure that we occidentals who live with our watches in our hands can determine precisely the values of time words in ancient times or oriental lands. Moreover, Jesus did not speak Greek, but Aramaic; and we do not know of what Aramaic word the Greek *aionios* is a translation, nor what its time value was in the elastic and picturesque speech of Palestine. We do know from ancient literature that the longest time-words were used with great flexibility. Jonah speaks of his three days' imprisonment as "forever" because it seemed to him a long time.

The other argument is this. "The Bible uses the same adjectives for the timelessness of both heaven and hell. If you show that hell is not inevitably eternal, you show that heaven also is not eternal." That is not true. There might be an official report of social conditions in Chicago or New York which would say that we must reckon with both the brothel and the church as permanent elements in our city's life. The same word "permanent" might be used, and properly, in such a report. Yet there might be a million reasons why the brothel ought to go and the church not, and that very report might concern itself with plans for the ultimate elimination of the brothel.

If you were a minister, you would have to bury all sorts and conditions of people, good people and murderers, little children and wayward youth.

247

Sometimes a mother would come to you and ask about her boy who had died. She would say, "He was wayward, but he was not wholly bad. He was kind; in many ways he was good; but he was not a Christian. Is it wicked for me to hope?" What would you tell her? I should tell her it would be wicked for her not to hope. I should tell her God loves her boy more than she does, and her own love is the reflection of God's love for him. I should not dare tell her more, nor would I dare tell her less. I do not know much about it. I only know that God is good, and I hope for every great and beautiful thing.

Does any man say, if what I have been saying is true, he will live sinfully here, and repent hereafter? I can not think any man who hears me is so contemptibly mean. But if you are thinking any such thing, do you suppose you can live a reckless, wilful life here, and come to the gate of heaven and find an angel there with a crown and harp for you, and you take it and go in and be happy? You could not look a respectable angel in the face. You would want to go like Judas and hang yourself. And when you stood in the presence of Him who

248

was crucified that He might save men, you would beat your breast and ask the privilege of slinking off to hell for a millennium or two, and then of scrubbing the golden streets for about a million years in the hope of some time becoming worthy of some very humble place in heaven. No, the logic of this chapter is this: You must reckon with the same God in whatever world you go to. If you go to hell, the most blistering fact that burns your consciousness will be the love of God. Since you must find Him wherever you go, and reckon with Him, do it now.

The Sybil offered Tarquin nine books at a price. He refused, and she destroyed three, and doubled the price. Still he refused, and she destroyed three more and again doubled the price, then he bought the three that remained. No man has ever called him wise, or supposed that he drove a shrewd bargain. No man acts wisely who postpones inevitable choices to an uncertain future, letting priceless opportunities go to waste.

There is a fine element of risk in the enterprises of God. There is a sublime appearance of uncertainty in the Divine undertakings. There is that

249

which fills the doubtful with a sense of the consciousness of success and throws into the sphere of the problematical a thrilling but trembling certainty. How can God be in hell? How can there be any hell? If there is a God what can be the meaning and function of hell? Of one thing we are certain. The love of God like a rainbow spans the blackest abyss made possible by human sin. It is inconceivable that God should cease to love; it is utterly impossible that the heart of God should become a stranger to pity.

Does it follow that there is hope in hell? Where there is life there is always hope. We dare not set limits to the compassion of God's everlasting mercy. But the thought of God's spirit as present in hell need not bring to us too swift an element of comfort. The presence of the spirit of God in the heart of the transgressor must ever be the keenest element in the Divine retribution. The men of the Apocalypse who called upon the rocks to fall and cover them are seeking to escape from the presence not of Satan but of God. It is his presence that causes the sharpest shame and the bitterest remorse. It is this which makes conscience so terrible to face.

What is conscience after all but the presence of God in human memory? What is it that drives men to confession or to suicide when they have no accuser but themselves? To the wilful transgressor, to the shameful impenitent the presence of God in hell can bring only keener sorrow, only more swift and sure and poignant self-condemnation.

And yet we need not shrink and must not shrink from the confident declaration that the presence of God is a ground of eternal hope. We have no authority whatever to say to any man that he can continue in sin and dying impenitent can make up in some future life for opportunities neglected here. On the other hand, we have no right to limit the mercy of God. Punishment is not arbitrary. God's grace is not vindictive. The love of God is a love not only unto the uttermost, but unto the nethermost. Punishment is for the sake of the good that God can do through punishment and can do in no other way.

> Deep below, as high above
> Swings the circle of God's love.

CHAPTER XIV

THE Protestant Reformation had its origin in a righteous protest against abuses then existing in the Roman Catholic Church. Among them, and chief among those that evoked the *Theses* of Luther, was that of the doctrine of Indulgences. The Pope was endeavoring to raise money for the completion of St. Peter's at Rome; and one of the ways of securing it was by the sale of Indulgences. Whatever the Roman Church itself intended to teach, those who had the sale of these Indulgences taught that by the purchase of them with money designated for so holy a cause, men might buy pardon from sin for themselves or their dead friends. The souls of the dead were and are held to go, not direct to heaven, but to an intermediate state called Purgatory, where they are purged from the sins of earth preparatory to their entrance into heaven.

252

They were held to have no power of earning money, but their living friends could contribute money, which, applied to the purchase of Papal Indulgences, had the effect of shortening the period of their sojourn in Purgatory and lessening its rigors.

Against this doctrine the Reformers protested with all their might; and in the reformed churches there was strong protest against any habit of prayer for the dead. This protest was intended as a safeguard against any recrudescence of the false doctrine of the value of purchased masses for the dead, and also as an expression of faith that the soul chooses in this life its eternal destiny.

But when these superstitions are laid aside, there is still something to be said for an intermediate state between earth and heaven. There are certain more or less obscure passages of Scripture which may be held to teach it. And beside this is a fact, that character as it exists in the life of men and women departing from this world, is not, in every instance, fit for immediate entrance into a perfected heaven.

For myself, I find no particular comfort in the

doctrine of an intermediate state, yet, we admit that many people who leave this world too good to deserve a place in hell are not fitted, so far as we can judge, for an immediate entrance into such a place as we believe heaven to be. Sam Jones, in his evangelistic sermons, was accustomed to say that if all people who expected to go to heaven really got there, he would need to adopt precautions for the protection of his valuables. There is no moral quality in the fact of death; no magic about it which can be expected suddenly to transform a crabbed or miserly or petulant Christian into an irreproachable angel. There are Christians who, for their own well-being and the comfort of their associates, will need a few millions of years of instruction if they are to live comfortably with other people in heaven.

I do not know who invented the notion that there can be no possible sin in heaven; that, as I once heard a man say, if St. Paul should commit in heaven one tiniest offense against the perfect will of God, he would be cast out and hurled into the bottomless pit. No one is wise enough to be justified in any such nonsense. There will be no sin in heaven, in the sense of lawless hostility to God; but souls in heaven will have to learn, and there will always be the possibility of learning by the making of mistakes and trying again.

Without committing ourselves to the clumsy and needless doctrine of an intermediate state, or the wholly useless machinery of a future probation, let us cherish the belief that heaven is capable of adjusting itself to people of many degrees of sanctity and experience; that it is a place of perpetual growth in knowledge and in grace and in the fine art of living together.

May we pray for our dead?

In Great Britain and other countries where loss of life was heavy in the World War, this question is asked with new insistence. There has been strong opposition in Puritan theology to the practise of prayer for the dead. It has seemed to suggest the idea of Purgatory, and has been opposed on the ground that those who are dead are either saved or lost, and our prayers can not avail for them. There is a growing conviction that this does not answer the agonized question of sorrowing hearts, and I think it does not.

Speaking for myself, I hold no theory of Purgatory, yet I see no good reason why we should not pray for our dead. We do not need to pray to God to be merciful toward them, for He is more merciful than we are, and loves our dear ones more than we do. The fact that our loved ones are in heaven is not the last word of our hope for them: we hope that there they still will grow in love and strength and goodness, and I do not know any reason to think that our prayers may not be a help to them. I am sure that we are under no obligation to cease loving them, and why should we cease to pray for them? If it is any comfort so to do, I am certain no one has a right to forbid it.

Death as we stand close to it seems a great and wide gulf between us and another world; it may not be nearly as wide as we think. You stand beside a river and look across; it is very wide, deep and dark. But if you climb a mountain and look down, it is just a narrow silver ribbon, and the two sides of it are not very unlike. So, I think, may be the two shores of the river of death as we shall look down from another world. But I believe the other shore is more fertile, more beautiful; and the same

256

God reigns on both sides. I think your prayers can bridge that stream; at least, if it comforts you to think so, you have the right to think so, and to pray.

Let me add this word of caution. If your heart impels you to pray for your dead, do not let your prayers degenerate into superstition in any form. It were better to leave our loved ones alone in the dignity of death than to let our childish fancy lead us into foolish and degraded forms of prayer for them. And do not pray any prayer which assumes either that your dead need your prayers to induce God to be kindly and generous and merciful to them, or that you need their prayers to God to induce Him to be merciful and gracious and just to you. If you will bear these cautions in mind, and you find comfort in prayer for those whom you have "loved long since and lost a while," no man has a right to forbid you.

CHAPTER XV

HEAVEN

THE word Heaven is used in the Bible in three distinct yet closely related senses: The first is the atmospheric heaven, the place of clouds, the home of the birds, the region in plain sight and a little beyond our reach. "The fowls of the heaven" live there. The second is the astronomical heaven, the region in which the sun and moon and planets move. The third is the theological heaven, the abode of God and of holy angels and of redeemed souls.

It is not to be supposed, however, that this division is arbitrary or constant. When Paul spoke of being caught up into the third heaven, it is not necessary to imagine that he carefully defined the two lower ones; much less is precise numeration essential when "the seventh heaven" is spoken of. The throne of God is exalted high above all visible objects.

We need not be disturbed by questions of direction or location. That heaven is conceived of as above need not interfere with our knowledge of the revolution of the earth. The elevation is spiritual, and not necessarily geographical.

Yet we are hardly justified in saying, "Heaven is a state and not a place." It is, to be sure, a state; and it can hardly be called a place in the sense that we are to demand its location at some particular point in the stellar map; but it is somewhere. "I go to prepare a place for you." Heaven is a prepared place for a prepared people. Where it is, and at what point in the earth's revolution we should think of it as nearest when we say that it is above, we need not trouble to ask. We are constrained in our thinking to locate it, and we think of it as above. That is all we need to say or to know of its location.

The doctrine of a future life has been abused, as most good things have been abused, in its use as a divine bribe upon the one hand and menace upon the other. We may well pray:

What conscience tells me should be done, ___
    Or warns me not to do,

259

That teach me more than hell to shun,
This more than heaven pursue.

But we do not need to regard it as a selfish reward of virtue that the coldly calculating Christian
shall barter joy in this world for greater joy hereafter, or avoid the sin which in his heart he loved for
fear of the hell he deserves. On this subject James
Freeman Clark spoke sane and wise words:

I know that it is the custom to say that belief in
immortality is not necessary to human virtue or
human happiness. The highest and noblest virtue,
it is declared, does not need the stimulus of future
reward and punishment. If there is no hereafter,
good men will continue to be good for the sake of
goodness. And, if there is no hereafter, men will
continue to enjoy this life because of its own interest. The earthly paradise is enough for us, it is
said: we need no future paradise.

This is partially true. Goodness may not need
future reward and punishment as a motive. But
the influence on life which immortality furnishes
does not act mainly as the expectation of reward.
We are made better, stronger, nobler, by our faith
in immortality, because we have around us the
mighty influence of the great cloud of witnesses
who have gone up. We belong to their world as
well as to our own. Is it nothing to know that the
spiritual universe above us is not empty, but full of

immortal souls, advancing on forever, in sympathy with all that is good here? Is it nothing to believe that the saints and martyrs of all time, the prophets and heroes of every age, are still full of the same powers, still devoted to the same generous activities? Will our lives be the same whether we believe that all the regions of being above man are full of intelligence, energy, and love, or that they are a vast emptiness, an infinite and inane void?

It is sometimes said that it is sheer egotism for any man to assume that he is so important to the universe that God must raise him from the dead and grant him life everlasting. It is said that we need not demand for our own selves or our loved ones identity of being in the life to come. It is affirmed that, having served his purpose with us here, God can better dispose of us when we die and begin again new life with new beings. But this does not satisfy the demands of affection, nor yet those of the higher reason. We are by no means sure that newly created beings without our experience and personality could serve God as well as men can serve.

There is no Scripture basis for the belief that angels were once human beings. They may have been, but if so the fact is not stated. If they be-

long to a different order, to a class that has never
known struggle such as we have had, heaven must
possess for them a pathetic lack of background.
William Hervey Woods with keen penetration has
set forth this truth,—in a poem entitled *Angels
and Men*:

> He said, "We have no kin—
> No angel of us sees with fond surprise
> Himself smile at him from his daughter's eyes,
>   And though new worlds we win,
> Lonely and chill is our white angel-hood
> Beside the warm, quick, quivering woof of blood
>   All men are knitted in;
> Envy us not our palace-pomp enskied,
> We have but heaven, and ye have home beside."
>
> He said, "We have no tears—
> But when mid our antiphonies, we mark
> Jehovah stoop, because down in your dark
>   Some sobbing prayer he hears,
> And with His own hand lift the weeper's head,
> To us who watch, so to be comforted
>   Outbids all griefs and fears,
> And Michael even would snatch at man's distress
> Might he but know man-wise God's gentleness."
>
> He said, "We have no scars,
> No knotted wounds Immanuel's touch may kiss
> To sudden-thrilling, keen, deep-seated bliss,
>   But wistful mid the stars

We stand, and hear Him speak rapt, shaken words
With His old comrades of the time of swords.
    O men, it is your wars
With Him and for Him, make the Christ your
    own—
You and your Jesus here have scars alone!"

The Bible descriptions of heaven have been vulgarized by too much literalism. Any description of happy existence and relationship of spiritual beings would of necessity employ figures of speech derived from pleasant objects in this life. It is not of heaven but of a regenerate society here on earth that the Book of Revelation speaks when it tells of golden streets and gates of pearls and harps and crowns. It is quite legitimate to use these figures also of heaven, provided we remember that we are not dealing with prose, and are speaking the language of illustration and not of definition. So soon as we make the Book of Revelation a kind of *Baedeker* of heaven, we become bound to a crass materialism, none the less pathetic because it is used in the service of religion.

Healthy boys and girls in this generation are not singing, "I want to be an angel," and healthy older people do not contemplate with strong and consistent desire the picture of a heaven of eternal lethargy, broken only by choir rehearsals.

Broadly speaking, we are justified in thinking that heaven will preserve all the essential values of human life, and protect them upon the field of a larger and nobler existence. Whatever helps the imagination to visualize this, will, if not morbidly dwelt upon, assist to make heaven a trifle more tangible.

Whatever is best in this life will be with us in heaven, or if not that, then something adapted to meet the same need, but better.

The saddest funerals are not those where the most tears are shed; the saddest are those where every one is secretly glad, and where there is only a hollow pretense of grief to satisfy the demands of public decency. Grief is the thorny stem on which bloom the fairest flowers of love. We could not suffer if we did not love.

It is not certainty but faith that upholds us in time of sorrow. There can be no complete demonstration of any of the finer things of life. Jonathan Brierley was no writer of cant, nor did he write much of heaven. His was a faith for the day's

work; but when he came to face death he did so
with the calm confidence that he knew whom he
had believed:

Death remains for us all a great venture. "Who
knows," says Euripides, "if life be death and death
life?" On that "Who knows," the great "Perhaps," countless multitudes of our fellow men have
been content to live and die. To us, with all the
light that comes from both science and religion, the
step from "here" to "there" we have all to take remains still a step into the unknown. The mystery
of living is kept up to its last moment. We are to
be on tiptoe all the time. The soul is not allowed to
support itself on any other material than faith.
And that it is so is surely well; for us it is best so.
Were certainty and clear vision better we should
have had it. But we are to trust the whole way and
go by trusting. We have been led too well and too
graciously to permit of our believing that we shall
be fooled at the last.

Faith in immortality is the highest tribute which
the mind of man has paid to the value of life.
When that faith is unselfish, intelligent and truly
religious, it is the highest and noblest form of expression of confidence in the fundamental sound-
ness of the universe and the eternal goodness of
God.

We shall not be satisfied to be told that our own loved ones are forever gone from us, but that God will give us other and compensating joys, for we want the assurance that the love of this life is not wasted. It is too precious a thing to lose with life. If it were thus to be lost, God would mercifully save us the bitterness of our grief. Grief is permitted, that comfort may be abundant.

God does not send us strange flowers every year;
When the spring winds blow o'er the pleasant
    places,
The same dear things lift up the same fair faces,
    The violet is here.

It all comes back, the odor, grace, and hue,
Each sweet relation of its life repeated;
Nothing is lost, no looking-for is cheated;
    It is the thing we knew.

So after the death winter it will be;
God will not put strange sights in heavenly places;
The old love will look out from the old faces;
    Loved one, I shall have thee.

The largest building Jesus ever saw on earth was the Temple at Jerusalem. It was a house of many rooms. When He journeyed thither with his par-

ents at the age of twelve, He asked, "Wist ye not
that I must be in my Father's house?" The same
idea which He used of the Temple on that occasion
is expressed in the word which He used of heaven
in his last discourse with his disciples, though in
Luke 2:49 the noun does not appear. As the temple in Jerusalem was a house of many rooms devoted to a wide variety of purposes, but all
constructed with reference to the promotion of a
common end, so also was His Father's house in
heaven: the eternal abode of the blessed.

Interesting as is his use of the word "house," the
word "mansions" is even more so. It suggests a
degree of privacy, an element of personal and social relationship belonging to heaven and absent, or
at least not emphasized, in the popular conception
of what that place may contain. When we get to
heaven we are not going to camp out-of-doors in
the golden streets, surrounded by a mob of angels.
Heaven has its sacred privacies; its companion-
ships free from the rude intrusion of celestial gos-
sip. I should not like to translate it, "My Father's
house is a great big apartment building," but that
would be nearer the truth than to make it read,

"My Father's house is a place where people do nothing but attend public functions of a religious nature."

It is interesting, too, that our Lord said, "I go to prepare." That kind of preparation was usually delegated to a servant. Peter and John had done that with respect to the very room where Jesus engaged in this conversation. They had gone to Jerusalem early in the afternoon to prepare the guest chamber for Jesus and his disciples who came in the evening. He told them that He was going to heaven to do there what two of his disciples had done for Him that very day. They had gone ahead to prepare a place for Him. They had come to Jesus asking, "Where wilt thou that we prepare for Thee to eat the Passover?" (Matthew 26:17.) He told them where to go and they had gone and prepared this very room. Now, He, using the very same word which they had used to Him, said, "I go and prepare a place for you." It is an interesting bit of reciprocity, but we must not dwell upon it, for our chief thought centers round another word, the word here translated "mansions."

The most interesting word in this verse and the

one which is the key to its real meaning is "mansions." It is a word which occurs in the New Testament as a noun only here and in a later verse in this same chapter, where Jesus says that He and the Father will enter into the lives of those who love Him, "and make our abode with him." (John 14:23.) But as a verb we have the word in a large number of passages; and we find it both as noun and verb in other Greek literature. By this process of comparison we discover that the word has no such settled and permanent connotation as the word "mansions." It is used of lodging places as where Jesus lodged with Zaccheus (Luke 19:5); and was asked to abide with the disciples (Luke 24:29). The same verb is used of Peter's lodging with Simon, the tanner (Acts 9:43); of Paul's boarding place with Aquilla and Priscilla (Acts 18:3), and of his visiting at Cæsarea "a good many days" (Acts 21; 7-8, 10).

It is interesting to discover in a reference like this an incidental but still fairly clear indication of one of the conditions of habit. So far as this verse gives us any light at all, its suggestion is that of progress. When we get to heaven we shall not settle down in everlasting stagnation; we shall move on.

We shall move on in knowledge. These minds of ours are not constructed for a sudden and explosive expansion, either on earth or in heaven. The soul itself is not a physical entity; it is our capacity for development. We struggle through this world with painfully little knowledge, but normal life never loses its capacity for growth and its eagerness to grow. We may reasonably assume that heaven will be a place of progress in the exact sciences, such as one quaint philosopher had in mind when being asked of the occupation of God through eternity, answered, "God geometrizes."

And yet it will be a minor interest of heaven that we shall discover in abstract pursuit; we shall grow in knowledge in heaven and that normally, as Jesus on earth grew in wisdom while He grew in stature. "Now we know in part; then shall we know even as also we are known."

We shall move on in our capacity for mutual helpfulness. Our whole mind and condition are constructed with reference to social relationship. We might as well expect to walk through heaven on one leg as to suppose that we shall go through with unsocial personality.

270

We shall grow in goodness. People sometimes assume that the instant we get to heaven every fault we have will be miraculously eradicated. I do not believe anybody knows that to be true. It seems to be the plan of God that we shall be permitted to make a good many blunders here on earth that we may learn by our mistakes. I know no reason why we should suppose that God will instantly and violently abrogate that method. I have heard people say that if the highest archangel in glory should commit one slightest sin that single violation of God's law would cast him instantly down to hell. Nobody knows that and I do not believe it. I think that God who is so patient with us here can afford to be and will be patient with us while we slowly but surely learn better.

I have already spoken of the fact that the only other place in the New Testament where the word "mansions" is used as a noun is in this same chapter, where Jesus says that He and the Father will make their abode with those who love God. That is a very precious promise, whose beginnings are available now and whose reach extends to the farther side of eternity. In heaven we shall be

moving on, but we shall always have companionship. The golden streets have other traffic than
the celestial moving vans. We move on, but our
Heavenly Father and our gracious Saviour move
on with us.

It is a satisfaction thus to be assured that in the
next world, as in this, "Our God goes marching
on." Progress does not halt, either on God's part
or ours. This urge in the blood of normal human
life is not wholly a manifestation of our human
restlessness; it is a manifestation of something in
the heart of God that from the days of Israel's
wanderings in the wilderness on through the tri-
umphal progress of heaven keeps God and us forever moving. The homing instinct of the soul that
drives us Godward is no more a normal part of our
nature than the adventurous push within us, spur-
ring us ever on to catch the rhythm of the Divine
music and keep step with God.

A good many years ago I had a visit by the road-
side with an unlettered preacher in the Kentucky
mountains. It was a hot day. We stopped to
water our horses where we crossed a stream and
then dismounted and sat for a little while upon the

bank. He first tried to interest me in a horse trade
and then proceeded to tell me of an illness which
he had experienced seven years before, which produced a remarkable change in him. It was typhoid
fever and for several weeks he was in delirium. He
told me that as a result of that sickness he found
himself for the first time in his life able to read the
Bible. He had attended school but a few weeks
in his childhood and learned a small number of
words out of Webster's blue-backed spelling book
according to the method of instruction then in
vogue in the mountain schools, but he never had put
words together until after his sickness, when to his
delight he found himself able to read the Bible. He
did not pretend to have become very efficient at it,
but by spelling out some words and skipping the
hardest ones, he had the indescribable joy of being
able to read his Bible. I do not doubt but that what
he told me was true, and his case is not without
parallel in the records of psychology.

But he also told me that he died. He was conscious all the time while his friends gathered about
him and prepared his body for burial. He heard
what they said and knew what they were doing and

could see his body and knew that it was no longer his, and it was a sorrow to him when finally he had to reinhabit it and make those involuntary manifestations of life which caused his friends to desist from their preparations for his burial. The doctor called it by some name he did not know and insisted that he never really had been dead, but he knew better. Now people said he was crazy when he told about it, but he knew that he was perfectly sane and describing his actual experience.

He went to heaven, so he said, and to his great surprise was not immediately ushered into the presence of all its joys; indeed he never got very far in. He was just in the first room, which was more beautiful than any he had ever seen. It was ceiled with plain lumber and painted a dove color and around him were beauties indescribable, but on the farther side was an unglazed window at a height where those in the first room could see through, and the next room was as much more beautiful than the first as the first room was than anything he had ever seen on earth. But even this was not the end, for he could see a similar window in the farther partition of the second room and had a suggestion of others in the rooms that were still beyond.

He said "They call me crazy and say the fever turned my head, but I know what I seen and it's so. You stay in the first room a thousand years and think it's only a day, for a thousand years are a day with the Lord, and it takes you that long to see all there is to see and learn all there is to learn in that first room. And it takes you longer in the next room, for it's more beautiful than the first and you never can get tired of it for you are always learning something you didn't know and seeing something more beautiful than you ever dreamed. And so you go on and on, room after room, and room after room, always learning, always finding out something, always increasing in your power to enjoy more beautiful things and you never get to the last one, for it's worlds without end. Amen."

I traveled in Palestine last year, and I was there also before the day of automobiles. I am always moved when I remember how our camp was struck each morning and ready for us in a distant place at night. Each morning at five o'clock the servants in the camp blew on instruments of discord, and pounded on pans and pots and basins and marched around the Jericho of our habitations, and the can-

vas walls of our abode fell down in just thirty
minutes after the first blast of the horn and bang
of the pan. If any of us had lingered in bed, and
was not dressed, it did him no good to shout in protest, for the morning toilet had to be finished in the
open. By the time we were seated for our break-
fast in the dining tent, we beheld our tents, beds
and baggage all loaded on mules and camels, moving away we knew not where. Neither did we see
it as we rode, for often it went another way.

We did not see our camp at noon, for we lunched
in the shade of trees if there were trees, or of walls
where there were no trees, and sometimes we found
the peaceful "shadow of a great rock in a weary
land."

But late in the afternoon as the sun was setting,
we rounded a turn in the road, or came to the top
of a hill, and there we saw our tents. And inside
of every several tent were the beds and basins and
the baggage all set and in waiting. It was a wel-
come sight. Never did we behold it without a thrill.

We live in a changing world, and here we have
no continuing city, but endeavor each day that we
may nightly pitch our moving tent a day's march

276

nearer home. Year by year we have seen much that we cared for that has moved on and left us puzzled and bewildered, and sometimes in tears.

But we know what another traveler meant whose name was once Saul, who is also called Paul, when he said in effect, We know that if our earthly house of this tent wherein we have our mortal life were stricken down and collapsed so that it seemed dissolved in nothingness, we have awaiting and prepared for us a building of God, a house not made by hands, in the place toward which we journey. Wherefore, we witness the moving forward of the things we love not without some sorrow and concern, but without utter dismay. For some time, when the day is near its ending, we shall pass through a valley that is shadowed but we shall go without fear. And this hope is for all who have like precious faith.

"Wherefore, comfort one another with these words."

I do not think we are in any danger of thinking of Heaven in terms too beautiful. All our thought must be in figures derived from this life, and is probably very inadequate. But the truth is **not** less than our faith. We are at liberty to believe the very best that we can think, for if God is our Father, and has planned this great gift for his children, then there is nothing too good to be true.

I was riding on a train from New York to Chicago. In the Pullman with me, among other passengers, rode a mother and a little girl of five. The little girl and I got acquainted. She had a set of dominoes, and we played a game of her own invention. We made beds. A domino stood on end made a headboard, and two dominoes laid flat made the mattress. We made single beds and double beds and twin beds. We tried to make beds such as the porter made up in the car, but we did not succeed so well.

She and her mother were on their way to South Bend. The little girl's father had gone on to take up a new position under the same firm for whom he previously worked in New York.

When we reached Elkhart, I said to the little girl, "This is Elkhart. It is one hundred and one miles from Chicago. This is our last long stop. Here we cut off the dining-car, and here, perhaps, we shall change engines. We run to Chicago in

278

two hours and twenty minutes, and South Bend comes before Chicago."

She said, "I don't care if this old train never gets to South Bend."

I inquired of her why she held South Bend in such low esteem, and she told me that it was because in South Bend she would be required to learn "very hard letters."

With a little investigation I learned these further facts: She had just started to go to school in New York in the middle of September, and had attended not more than three weeks when her mother received word that her father's position in South Bend was assured, and the removal followed. The little girl had heard her mother say that she was sorry to leave just then, as the little girl had just got nicely started in school, and now would have to begin all over again. The little girl understood this to mean that she would encounter in South Bend an entirely new alphabet, and she dreaded the "very hard letters."

Now, if any of you ever learned the English alphabet, you will not blame that little girl. If you have forgotten how hard it really is to commit to memory the forms and names and phonetic value of twenty-six arbitrary symbols, just learn another alphabet as a wholesome exercise—the Greek, or if you know that, the Hebrew. You may find the Greek moderately easy, for the letters are very similar to ours, but you will be thankful that the Hebrew alphabet has only twenty-two letters. This little girls had learned twenty-six letters, and a good many short words in three weeks, and when she thought of the necessity of learning another alphabet, she did not care whether the old train ever reached South Bend, for she dreaded the "very hard letters." Her memories of the difficulty of learning the alphabet were recent and vivid, and she had reason to dread the learning of other and possibly more difficult ones.

I told the little girl that I had journeyed through South Bend a hundred times, and that I had reliable information that she would not need to learn any new alphabet. I told her that the same twenty-six letters were employed there, and that the spelling was identical with that used in New York. I told her that very few people in South Bend spelled c-o-w with a "k"; that it was not considered good form; and that d-o-g and c-a-t were spelled exactly as they were in New York.

I succeeded in convincing her, and the information comforted her. She grew more interested in the approach of the end of the journey, and I think she appreciated my great knowledge of the state of education in South Bend.

It is in some such way I like to think of the relations of this life to that which is to come. Our education here is just begun, and we find ourselves caught up out of this kindergarten of the soul and taken to where it seems everything will be strange and we shall have to begin all over again. I wonder if our Heavenly Father has not some experienced angels who have nothing better to do than to meet us somewhere near the terminal, and tell us better.

Kind deeds, and loving words, and helpful acts, and noble aspirations, and worthy resolves, and heroic faith, and struggles to overcome temptation, and desires to serve others, are the alphabet, the primary forms, out of which, I am confident, all the words in the unabridged dictionary of the language of heaven are to be spelled. I do not think that heaven is very far away, or that our friends who have gone before us are remote, or that our life here is of no concern to them, or theirs to us. I believe that there is a community of interest; that we are to use the standards of that life as the measure of this when we pray, "Thy kingdom come, as in Heaven, so on earth," and that we are to use the experiences of this life as having permanent significance in their relation to the life of the Kingdom of God.

This is my own faith, the faith which helps me, and the faith which in the hour of sorrow I bring for the comfort of those who mourn. It is a faith that has its deep springs in the noblest and best aspirations of human life, and its assurance of validity in the promises of the Word of God. It has the attestation of the Lord Jesus, who as He entered the tomb and made it radiant with the hope of immortality, said to his disciples, "If it were not so, I would have told you."

The train stopped at South Bend, and the little girl waved me a farewell.

When I last saw her she was in the arms of her father.

THE END